THE OTHER

matchbox
TOYS

IDENTIFICATION & VALUE GUIDE

1947 – 2004

DANA JOHNSON

Models of Yesteryear
King Size
Major Pack
Skybusters
and more...

COLLECTOR BOOKS
A Division of Schroeder Publishing Co., Inc.

On the front cover:
1906 Rolls Royce, Models of Yesteryear, Y-10 (top left)
Transport Helicopter, 2003 Skybusters (top right)
GMC Hopper Train, Major Pack M-4, King Size K-4 (center left)
Messerschmitt KR200, Matchbox Collectibles VEM-04 (center right)
Daffy Duck 4x4 Pickup, Matchbox character toy (bottom left)
Harley-Davidson Electraglide Motorcycle and Sidecar, 1:10 scale, Harley-Davidson series #76310

On the back cover:
BP Auto Tanker, Major Pack M-1 (top left)
1948 Tucker Torpedo, Matchbox Collectibles, Barrett-Jackson Collection (top right)
Bentley R-type Continental, The Dinky Collection DY-13 (below 1948 Tucker Torpedo)
Foden Ready-Mix Concrete Truck, King Size K-13 (center left)
1957 BMW 507, Matchbox Collectibles Y-33 (center right)
1967 Pontiac GTO, Matchbox Collectibles, Muscle Cars YMC-03 (below Foden Ready-Mix truck)
Big Bird's Fire Engine, Matchbox character toy (bottom left)

Cover design by Beth Summers
Book design by Allan Ramsey

Collector Books

P.O. Box 3009

Paducah, KY 42002-3009

www.collectorbooks.com

Copyright © 2005 Dana Johnson

The current values indicated in this book should be used only as a guide. They are not intended to set prices, which vary from one section of the country to another. Auction prices as well as dealer prices vary and are affected by condition as well as demand. Neither the author nor the publisher assumes responsibility for any losses that might be incurred as a result of consulting this guide. Any errors or omissions are strictly the responsibility of the author.

The following are registered trademarks of Mattel, Inc.: MATCHBOX, MATCHBOX COLLECTIBLES, SUPER-FAST, LASER WHEELS, LASERTRONICS, LIGHTNING, WORLD CLASS, SUPER GT, TWO PACK, TWIN PACK, TRAILERS, CONVOY, HIGHWAY EXPRESS, TEAM CONVOY, TEAM MATCHBOX, SKYBUSTERS, MAJOR PACK, KING SIZE, SPEED KINGS, SUPER KINGS, MATCHBOX MILITARY, BATTLE KINGS, SEA KINGS, ADVENTURE 2000, MODELS OF YESTERYEAR, DINKY, ROLAMATICS, and others.

DAYS OF THUNDER is a copyrighted trademark licensed by Paramount Pictures. INDY 500 and INDIANAPOLIS 500 are licensed from IMS Corp. PETERBILT, KENWORTH, KW, and AERODYNE are licensed trademarks of Paccar, Inc., Bellevue, Washington. GOODYEAR is a trademark of Goodyear Tire and Rubber Company. JEEP is a trademark of the Chrysler Corporation. ROLLS ROYCE is a trademark of Rolls Royce, Ltd. CATERPILLAR and CAT are licensed trademarks of Caterpillar Tractor Company. Other trademarks have been used with permission.

Contents

Preface 4

About the Author 4

Guide to Determining Values 5

Alphabetical Guide to Values and Variations 6

    Part 1: Action Series, Adventure 2000, Battle Kings, The Dinky Collection, King Size, LA Wheels, Major Pack, Matchbox Collectibles, Matchbox Military, Models of Yesteryear, Specials, Speed Kings, Super Kings, Turbo Specials 6

    Part 2: Two Packs, Twin Packs, Trailers, Matchmates, 900 Series Long Haul (TP-), Convoy, Super Rigs (CY-), Highway Express (HE-) 61

    Part 3: Other Matchbox Vehicles – Sea Kings, Skybusters, Star Cars 77

    Part 4: Matchbox Dolls and Action Figures, Toys and Games 87

Matchbox Ads 89

Resources 110

1948 Tucker Torpedo, Matchbox Collectibles, see pg. 58.

Preface

Since 1953, Matchbox toys have captured the hearts, minds, and imaginations of children around the world. As those children grew up, they remembered the fun and fascination they had for those little toys. As adults, they were transformed into Matchbox collectors.

From their humble beginnings in 1947 in a burned out London pub, partners Leslie and Rodney Smith built a lasting legacy to their ingenuity and entrepreneurial spirit through their Lesney Products Company and their Matchbox brand of diecast toys. Over 50 years and several owners later, Matchbox toys remain some of the worlds' most popular toys and collectibles.

This book is the result of author Dana Johnson's half century of fascination for these wonderful toys. His first book on Matchbox toys was published in 1994 to fill a void in the collector's reference library. He has since produced three more books on the subject, the latest of which is *Matchbox Toys, 1947 to 2004, 4th Edition*. The key difference between this latest effort and the rest is that *Matchbox Toys, 4th Edition* book is arranged alphabetically. Because of the enormity of the fourth edition's content, it was possible to list only those models that fell into a certain category. These Matchbox toys have been alternately called "the 1-75 series," or "the basic series," and encompass those models best known as Matchbox toys.

This new book deals with the rest of the line of toys that carried the Matchbox name but were not so closely identified with the brand. Besides covering the Major Pack series, King Size, Models of Yesteryear, Matchbox Collectibles, and The Dinky Collection from Matchbox, along with Skybusters, Convoy and more, this book also provides information on many other Matchbox toys not generally associated with the brand name, such as dolls, action figures, games, and other toys.

About the Author

Dana Johnson has enjoyed collecting and studying Matchbox toys since 1962, when he was seven years old. Originally from Skandia, Michigan, he has lived in several other places in Michigan until moving to Bend, Oregon, in 1985. He has lived there ever since.

His interest in diecast toys has since expanded to many other brands besides Matchbox, including Majorette, Tomica, Siku, Hot Wheels, Bburago, Maisto, Yatming, and hundreds of other brands. He has discovered so many brands of automotive toys and models (over 800) that he has written a book on them titled *Toy Car Collector's Guide*, available from Collector Books, your favorite bookstore, or from the author for $19.95 retail plus shipping and handling.

While holding down a full-time job, Dana also finds time to produce *Toy Car Collector Magazine* for his club, the Toy Car Collectors Association. He also maintains a worldwide website at www.toynutz.com through his home-based business, Dana Johnson Enterprises.

In addition, he has written several self-published books, including *Tomica — Japan's Most Popular Diecast Toys*, *Siku Toys of Germany*, *Majorette Toys of France*, and others. For a catalog of book titles and membership rates, send two first class stamps to:

Dana Johnson Enterprises
P. O. Box 1824
Bend, OR 97709-1824
24 hr. message phone: 541-318-7176
e-mail: toynutz@earthlink.net
website: www.toynutz.com

Guide to Determining Values

Values indicated in this book generally represent the average value for a given model. Although collectors are often willing to pay top dollar, occasionally even higher than book value, for models in new, or "mint," condition, especially when in original box or package, it is often possible to purchase models for considerably less. In the same spirit, you will often need to sell a model, and particularly an entire collection, at a much lower price than indicated by this or any book, since buyers of entire collections usually wish to quickly sell individual models at a reasonable profit. It is also important to know that most dealers will not buy toys in less than near mint condition.

For standardization, all values mentioned in this book are for models in new condition in original container. Two values are provided. The first value is for models in new condition but without original container; the second value is for model in its original container. The chart below is intended to assist in determining value on less-than-mint-condition toys. Note that "mint condition" denotes a model with no wear, no chips, no flaws. Models in a sealed blisterpack, for instance, may sometimes suffer wear from rubbing on the insides of the plastic blister and are therefore considered less-than-mint condition. So not everything still in the package should automatically be considered "mint."

Percent of Book Value	Evaluation
100%	Mint condition with original container
90 – 95%	Mint condition without container
80 – 85%	Near mint condition, close inspection reveals minor wear
70 – 75%	Excellent condition, visible minor wear
25 – 35%	Very good condition, visible wear, all parts intact
7 – 10%	Good condition, excessive wear, paint chipped or heavily worn
4 – 5%	Fair condition, parts broken or missing
2 – 3%	Poor condition, paint worn off, parts broken or missing
0.5 – 1%	Salvage for parts only

Alphabetical Guide to Values and Variations

Part 1: Action Series, Adventure 2000, Battle Kings, The Dinky Collection, King Size, LA Wheels, Major Pack, Matchbox Collectibles, Matchbox Military, Models of Yesteryear, Specials, Speed Kings, Super Kings, Turbo Specials

Since models in various series, particularly Models of Yesteryear, Matchbox Collectibles, and The Dinky Collection, have been interchanged from one series to the other, it is difficult to determine under which category you might find a particular model listed. It is for that reason that the list below combines all of these larger scale series models into an alphabetical listing. For organizational purposes, the arrangement below is by vehicle make and model, not by year. Vehicle year or vintage immediately follows make and model when provided. Year of introduction is at the end of the description of each model.

The Major Pack series was started by Lesney Products in 1957 in an attempt to capture a new market by producing larger, more detailed models than the regular so-called 1-75 series.

In 1960 Lesney introduced a similar series called King Size that ultimately replaced the Major Pack models. A few Major Pack models, however, survived the demise of the series in 1967 by being converted to King Size models. M-8 Guy Warrior car Transporter became K-8, M-4 GMC Tractor with Hopper Train became K-4, and M-6 Racing Car Transporter became K-5.

When the regular series was converted to Superfast, King Size became Speed Kings series. Later this series was reintroduced as Super Kings. Super Kings no longer exist as they have been incorporated into the Dinky Collection and Matchbox Collectibles series.

The Super Kings series was followed, after the test market of Matchbox Military in Germany and South Africa in 1973, by Battle Kings in 1974. Then came Sea Kings, and the futuristic Super Kings Adventure 2000 which was introduced in 1977. In 1991, the King Size series was renamed Action Series and divided into Action Farm, Construction, Emergency, and Super Kings. By then, the Matchbox Collectibles line was being developed, and eventually many models from the Yesteryear, Dinky, and King Size series, as well as from the 1-75 series, were incorporated into the new line.

For more easily locating a vehicle by make, the model year is listed following the model's name so that all examples are listed together by make and model, rather than by year.

AC Mack (see **Mack Model AC Truck**)

A.E.C. S Type Omnibus, 1922, Models of Yesteryear Y-23, introduced in 1982; Matchbox Collectibles European Transports YET-05, introduced in 1996
    1. "Haig," brown, Y-23 . . . .$18 – 24
    2. "Kennedy's," green, YET-05 . . . .$24 – 32
    3. "Lifebuoy Soap," blue, Y-23 . . . .$14 – 18
    4. "Maples Furniture," red, Y-23 . . . .$18 – 24
    5. "Rice Krispies," brown, Y-23 . . . .$18 – 24
    6. "Schweppes Tonic Water," red with dark brown
       interior, red wheels, Y-23 . . . .$20 – 30
    7. "Schweppes Tonic Water," red with light tan
       interior, red wheels, Y-23 . . . .$18 – 24
    8. "The RAC," red, Y-23 . . . .$18 – 24

A.E.C. Y Type Lorry, 1916, Models of Yesteryear Y-6, introduced in 1958
    1. dark gray with black plastic wheels . .$1,250 – 1,400
    2. dark gray with metal wheels . . . .$90 – 100
    3. light gray with metal wheels . . . .$80 – 90

Ahrens-Fox N-S-4 Fire Engine, 1927, 7", Matchbox Collectibles Fire Engine Collection . . . .$30 – 40

Ahrens-Fox Quad Fire Engine, 1930, YSFE-01, Matchbox Collectibles Fire Engine Collection, introduced in 1994, red with wooden stand . . . .$90 – 120

Aircraft Transporter (also see **Scammell Aircraft Transporter, Army Aircraft Transporter**)

Aircraft Transporter, 8", King Size K-13, 1976
    1. metallic gray, white airplane
       with no labels . . . .$18 – 24
    2. metallic gray, white airplane
       with stripes . . . .$18 – 24
    3. red, white airplane with "X4" label . . .$18 – 24
    4. red, brown airplane with "12" label,
       white wings . . . .$20 – 30

Airport Fire Tender (see **Airport Rescue Fire Tender**)

Airport Rescue Fire Tender, 5 5/16", King Size K-75, 1980
 1. yellow, "Airport Fire Tender" . . . .$14 – 18
 2. yellow, "Securite Aeroport,"
   France issue . . . .$60 – 80
 3. yellow, "Flughafan-Feurwehr," Germany
   issue . . . .$40 – 60

Albion 6-Wheeler, 1938, Models of Yesteryear
Y-42, introduced in 1991 . . . .$18 – 24

Allchin Traction Machine, 1926, Models of Yesteryear
Y-1, introduced in 1956
 1. diagonal red painted treads, copper
   boiler door . . . .$75 – 90
 2. diagonal red painted treads, gold
   boiler door . . . .$75 – 90

 3. diagonal unpainted treads,
   copper boiler door . . . .**$90 – 100**
 4. diagonal unpainted treads, gold
   boiler door . . . .$85 – 100
 5. diagonal unpainted treads, silver
   boiler door . . . .$125 – 150
 6. straight unpainted treads, copper
   boiler door . . . .$125 – 150
 7. smooth unpainted treads, gold
   boiler door . . . .$500 – 600

Allis-Chalmers Earth Scraper, 5⅞", King Size
K-6, 1961 . . . .$100 – 125

Ambulance (also see **DAF Ambulance**)

Ambulance, 4⅜", King Size K-49, 1973
 1. red with ivory roof, white interior, "Malteser,"
   Germany issue . . . .$35 – 50
 2. white with red roof, red interior,
   "Ambulance" . . . .$14 – 18
 3. white with red roof, white interior,
   "Ambulance" . . . .$20 – 30

AMC Javelin (see **Javelin AMX**)

American General Locomotive, 1862, Models of
Yesteryear Y-13, introduced in 1959

 1. dark green . . . .**$70 – 85**
 2. light green . . . .$300 – 350

AMX Javelin (see **Javelin AMX**)

Animal Transporter, 12 5/16", King Size
   K-8, 1980 . . . .$25 – 40

Armored Car Transporter, 7½", Matchbox Military MM-2
(South Africa and Germany only), 1973 . . . . . .$16 – 20

Army Aircraft Transporter, 8", Battle Kings
   BK-114, 1977 . . . .$45 – 60

Army Ambulance (see **DAF Ambulance**)

Army Helicopter (see **Kaman Seasprite Army Helicopter**)

Army Petrol Tanker, 9", Battle Kings
   BK-115, 1977 . . . .$60 – 85

Army Tank (see **M48A2 Tank, Chieftain Tank, King Tiger Tank**)

Articulated Container Truck (see **Scammell Articulated Container Truck**)

Articulated Horse Box (see **Dodge Articulated Horse Box**)

Articulated Petrol Tanker, 8", Matchbox Military MM-1
   (South Africa and Germany only), 1973 . .$16 – 24

Articulated Tipper Truck, 8", King Size K-18, 1974
1. dark blue cab, "Hoch & Tief,"
   Germany issue . . . .$50 – 70
2. metallic red cab . . . .$20 – 30
3. metallic silver cab . . . . . .$20 – 30
4. red cab . . . .$20 – 30
5. white cab, "Condor" . . . .$50 – 70
6. yellow cab . . . .$20 – 30

Aston-Martin DB4, 1960, DYB-06, introduced in 1998
1. metallic gray . . . .$24 – 32

Atkinson Logger, Matchbox Collectibles Steam-Powered Vehicles Collection . . . .$24 – 32

Atkinson Steam Wagon, 1918, Matchbox Collectibles Age of Steam YAS-10, introduced in 1997
1. "City of Westminster Works, Sewers
   & Highways" . . . .$30 – 45

Atkinson Steam Wagon, 1920, Models of Yesteryear Y-18, introduced in 1986; Matchbox Collectibles "Great Beers of the World" Collection YGB-03, YGB-22, introduced in 1996
1. "Beamish Special Stout Cork," YGB-22 . .$18 – 24
2. "Blue Circle Portland Cement,"
   yellow, Y-18 . . . .$18 – 24
3. "Burghfield Mills Reading," red, Y-18 . .$18 – 24
4. "Sand & Gravel," green, Y-18 . . . .$20 – 30

5. "The Swan Brewery Co. Ltd.,"
green, YGB-03 . . . .$18 – 24

Auburn 851 Boattail Speedster, 1933, Models of Yesteryear Y-19, introduced in 1980
1. khaki and beige with silver disc wheels,
   whitewall tires . . . .$20 – 30

2. khaki and beige with red disc wheels,
whitewall tires . . . . **$18 – 24**

3. cream with red disc wheels . . . .$18 – 24
4. white with blue side accents, blue
   spoked wheels . . . .$20 – 30
5. beige and cream with chrome
   spoked wheels . . . .$20 – 30

Audi Quattro, King Size K-95, 1982

1. metallic blue . . . .**$10 – 14**
2. metallic gray . . . .$10 – 14
3. white, "Audi Sport" . . . .$12 – 16
4. white, "Pirelli," "Duckhams" . . . .$9 – 12

Austin / BMW / Rosengart Special Limited Edition Set:
1928 Austin, 1928 BMW Dixi, 1928 Rosengart, Models of Yesteryear Y-65, introduced in 1992 . . . .$50 – 60

Austin 7, 1959, introduced in 1997

1. red . . . . **$24 – 32**

Austin A40, 1953, The Dinky Collection DY-15, introduced in 1990
1. "Brooke Bond Tea," red . . . .$12 – 16
2. "Dinky Toys," yellow . . . .$12 – 16
3. "Matchbox at Rugby," yellow,
   approximately 50 produced . . . . .$600 – 800

Austin Healy 100, 1956, The Dinky Collection DY-30, introduced in 1992; DYG-04, introduced in 1998
1. cream . . . .$24 – 32
2. dark green . . . .$18 – 24

Austin Mini Cooper S, The Dinky Collection DY-21, introduced in 1991
    1. cream with black roof . . . .$12 – 16

Austin Van 4-Vehicle Christmas Treasures Set
    1. YCC-01, introduced in 1994 . .$60 – 80 boxed set
    2. YCC-02, introduced in 1995 . .$30 – 40 boxed set
    3. YCC-03, introduced in 1996 . .$24 – 32 boxed set

Auto Tanker (see **BP Auto Tanker**)

Aveling Barford Tractor Shovel, 4⅛", King Size K-10, 1963
    1. blue-green, black plastic tires on silver
        metal hubs . . . .$90 – 120
    2. blue-green, black plastic tires on red
        plastic hubs . . . .$90 – 120

Aveling Porter Steam Roller, 1920, approximately 3", Models of Yesteryear Y-11, introduced in 1958 . .$65 – 80

Aveling Porter Steam Roller, 1920, approximately 4", Models of Yesteryear Y-21, introduced in 1987
    1. green with gray roof, inscription
        underneath roof . . . .$20 – 30
    2. green with gray roof, no inscription
        underneath roof . . . .$275 – 325

B Type London Bus (see **London Bus, 1911 B Type**)

Bandalero, 4½", King Size K-36, 1972 . . . .$14 – 18

Barracuda, 4¼", King Size K-51, 1973
    1. blue . . . .$14 – 18
    2. white . . . .$16 – 20

Bazooka, 4⅜", King Size K-44, 1973
    1. "Bazooka" labels . . . .$14 – 18
    2. "Firestone" labels . . . .$16 – 20

Bedford Articulated Truck (see **Bedford Ice Cream Truck**)

Bedford Courier Car Transporter, 10⁵⁄₁₆", King Size K-10, 1981 . . . .$20 – 30

Bedford Emergency Van, King Size K-143, 1987 .$9 – 12

Bedford Fire Tanker, YFE-04, Matchbox Collectibles Fire Engine Collection, introduced in 1995
    1. red, "Belrose Volunteer Bush Fire Brigade,"
        Australia issue . . . .$90 – 120
    2. red, no markings . . . .$35 – 50

Bedford Fire Truck, 1939, Matchbox Collectibles Fire Engine Collection YFE-17, introduced in 1997
    1. "City of Manchester Fire Brigade" . . . .$35 – 50

Bedford Ice Cream Truck, 4⁵⁄₁₆", Major Pack M-2, 1957
    1. "Wall's Ice Cream," metal wheels . .$150 – 200

  **2. "Wall's Ice Cream," gray plastic
    wheels** . . . .$150 – 200

Bedford KD Truck, 1939, Models of Yesteryear Y-63, introduced in 1992 . . . .$25 – 40

Bedford Pickup, Matchbox Collectibles "Great Beers of the World" Collection YGB-24, introduced in 1996
    1. "Toohey's" . . . .$18 – 24

Bedford Tractor and York Trailer, 4⅝", Major Pack M-2, 1961
    1. "Davies Tyres," orange cab, orange trailer base
        and doors, gray plastic tires . . . . . .$475 – 525
    2. "Davies Tyres," orange cab, orange trailer base
        and doors, black plastic tires . . . . .$150 – 200
    3. "LEP," silver cab, maroon trailer base and
        doors, black plastic tires . . . .$475 – 525
    4. "LEP," silver cab, black trailer base and doors,
        black plastic tires . . . .$150 – 200
    5. "LEP," silver cab, black trailer base, orange
        doors, black plastic tires . . . .$150 – 200

Bentley 4.5 Litre Supercharged, 1929, Models of Yesteryear Y-5, introduced in 1962

  1. metallic green . . . .$40 – 60
    2. metallic apple green . . . .$375 – 400
    3. silver plated . . . .$60 – 70

Bentley 4.5 Litre Supercharged, 1930, Models of Yesteryear Y-2, introduced in 1984
    1. dark blue . . . .$14 – 18
    2. dark green . . . .$14 – 18
    3. purple . . . .$18 – 24

Bentley LeMans, 1929, Models of Yesteryear Y-5, introduced in 1958
    1. gray tonneau . . . .$150 – 175
    2. green tonneau . . . .$65 – 80

Bentley R-Type Continental, 1955, The Dinky Collection DY-13, introduced in 1990

    1. metallic dark blue . . . .**$18 – 24**
    2. metallic light blue . . . .$12 – 16

Benz Fire Engine, 1912, Matchbox Collectibles Fire Engine Collection YFE-20, introduced in 1998 . .$35 – 50

Benz Limousine, 1910, Models of Yesteryear Y-3, introduced in 1966; Medallion Series YMS-02, introduced in 1996
    1. cream with green roof, green seats and grille,
       high cast headlights . . . .$40 – 60
    2. cream with green roof, green seats and grille,
       low cast headlights . . . .$30 – 40
    3. cream with green roof, red seats and grille,
       high cast headlights . . . .$40 – 60
    4. cream with pale lime green roof, green
       seats and grille . . . .$125 – 150
    5. cream with pale lime green roof, red
       seats and grille . . . .$125 – 150
    6. black with blue sides, black roof,
       brown grille . . . .$20 – 30
    7. dark blue with gold pinstripe trim,
       YMS-02 . . . .$20 – 30

    8. dark green with black roof, red grille .**$18 – 24**

    9. dark green with black roof, green grille $20 – 30
    10. dark green with lime green roof . . . .$50 – 60
    11. light green with black roof . . . .$20 – 30
    12. light green with green roof . . . .$60 – 75
    13. light green with pale lime green roof .$30 – 45

Berlin Bus (see **The Londoner**)

Bertone Runabout, 4", King Size K-31, 1972
    1. orange with green windows . . . .$14 – 18
    2. orange with clear windows . . . .$16 – 20

Big Tipper, 4¹¹⁄₁₆", King Size K-4, 1974 . . . .$15 – 20

Blaze Trailer Fire Chief's Car, 4", K-40, 1973 . .$14 – 18

BMW 507, 1957, Models of Yesteryear Y-21, introduced in 1988; Matchbox Collectibles Y-33, introduced in 1998
    1. blue, Y-21 . . . .$20 – 30

    2. beige, Y-33 . . . .**$35 – 50**

BMW 7-Series, King Size K-147, 1988
    1. black . . . .$8 – 10
    2. metallic gray, white and black interior, Ultra
       Class, China cast . . . .$16 – 20
    3. metallic gray, black interior, China cast . .$8 – 10

    4. metallic light blue, Macau cast . . . . . .**$8 – 10**
    5. metallic light blue, China cast . . . .$8 – 10
    6. red, China cast, Australia issue . . . . . .$20 – 30

BMW 7-Series Police Car, King Size K-154, 1988; Emergency EM-4, 1991 . . . .$9 – 12

BMW Motorcycle and Rider, 4⁵⁄₁₆", King Size K-82, 1981

1. metallic gray . . . .$14 – 18
2. black, "Polizei," Germany issue . . . . .$20 – 30

BMW Police Car, King Size K-142, 1987 . . . .$9 – 12

Boat Transporter (see **Power Boat and Transporter**)

BP Auto Tanker, 4", Major Pack M-1, 1961

1. **yellow and green with "BP" decals,**
   black plastic tires . . . .**$50 – 75**

Brabham BT 44B, 4¼", King Size K-41, 1977; K-72 1980
1. red, "Martini-Brabham," 7", K-41 . . . . .$14 – 18
2. red, "Martini-Brabham," 7", K-72 . . . . .$14 – 18
3. blue-green, K-72 . . . .$15 – 20

Breakdown Tow Truck, 5", King Size K-11, 1976
1. red, "Falck Zonen," Switzerland issue . .$80 – 110
2. yellow, "AA" . . . .$14 – 18
3. yellow, "Shell Recovery" . . . .$14 – 18

Bridge Transporter, 13⅛", King Size K-44, 1981 .$120 – 150

Bugatti Royale, 1930, Models of Yesteryear Y-45,
introduced in 1991 . . . .$18 – 24

Bugatti Type 35, 1923, Models of Yesteryear Y-6, introduced in 1961
1. blue with red dash and floor, black tires,
   gold grille . . . .$30 – 40
2. blue with red dash and floor, black tires,
   blue grille . . . .$75 – 85
3. blue with red dash and floor,
   gray tires . . . .$100 – 120
4. blue with white dash and floor . . . .$135 – 155

5. **red with black dash and floor** . . . . .**$135 – 150**

6. red with white dash and floor . . . . . .$30 – 50

Bugatti Type 44, 1927, Models of Yesteryear Y-24,
introduced in 1983
1. black with black interior, yellow
   accents . . . .$20 – 30
2. black with tan interior, red accents . . .$18 – 24
3. black with tan interior, yellow accents .$14 – 18
4. gray with tan interior, plum accents . . .$20 – 30

Bugatti Type 51, 1932, Models of Yesteryear Y-11,
introduced in 1987
1. blue . . . .$14 – 18

Buick Skylark Convertible, 1953
1. light blue, The Dinky Collection DY-29,
   introduced in 1992 . . . .$18 – 24
2. light green, DYM-37798 . . . .$40 – 50

3. **pale yellow, DYG-04, introduced in 1996** . .**$18 – 24**
4. pale yellow, Matchbox Collectibles Oldies
   but Goodies I, issued 2004 . . . .$9 – 12

Buick Special, 1958; DYG-11, introduced in 1998;
Matchbox Collectibles Oldies but Goodies II
1. metallic teal, DYG-11 . . . .$20 – 30
2. metallic teal, Oldies but Goodies II . . . .$9 – 12

Building Transporter, 5¾", King Size K-13, 1971 . .$20 – 30

Burrel Traction Engine, 1912, Matchbox Collectibles
Age of Steam YAS-08, introduced
in 1997 . . . .$25 – 40

Busch Steam Fire Engine, 1905, Models of Yesteryear Y-43, introduced in 1991; YSFE-03, Matchbox
Collectibles Fire Engine Collection, introduced in
1996
1. Y-43 . . . .$50 – 60
2. YSFE-03 . . . .$60 – 70

Cadillac, 1913, Models of Yesteryear Y-6, introduced
in 1967
1. gold plated . . . .$150 – 175
2. green . . . .$24 – 32

11

3. metallic gold, "1913" on base ......$20 – 30
4. metallic gold, "1913" on base ......$50 – 60
5. silver plated ....$125 – 150

Cadillac 452 V-16, 1933, Models of Yesteryear Y-34, introduced in 1990; Matchbox Collectibles Cars of the Rich & Infamous DYM35181, introduced in 1999
  1. dark blue ....$18 – 24
  2. dark green ....$30 – 40
  3. white ....$18 – 24

Cadillac Convertible, 1959, DYG-05, introduced in 1996
  1. black ....$18 – 24

Cadillac Coupe DeVille, 1959, The Dinky Collection DY-7, introduced in 1989; Matchbox Collectibles Budweiser Sports Cars DYM-37597, introduced in 1999
  1. "Coca-Cola," Matchbox Collectibles
    Coca-Cola Collection, 1:43 ....$12 – 18
  2. black, Matchbox Collectibles Oldies
    but Goodies I ....$9 – 12
  3. Golf, DYM-37597 ....$30 – 40
  4. pale blue, DY-7 ....$20 – 30
  5. pink, DY-7 ....$18 – 24

Cadillac Eldorado, 1953, DYG-13, introduced in 1998; Matchbox Collectibles Oldies but Goodies II, issued 2004
  1. black with white roof, DYG-13 ......$20 – 30
  2. black with white roof, Oldies but
    Goodies II ....$9 – 12

Cadillac Fire Engine, 1933, Models of Yesteryear
  1. Y-61, introduced in 1992 ....$20 – 30

2. YFE-03, Matchbox Collectibles Fire Engine Collection, introduced in 1994 .....$25 – 30

Cadillac V-16 (see **Cadillac 452 V-16**)

Camaro (see **Chevrolet Camaro**)

Cambuster, 4⅜", King Size K-43, 1973
  1. yellow with black base, amber windows ..$14 – 18
  2. yellow with black base, clear windows ..$14 – 18
  3. yellow with black base, green windows ..$14 – 18
  4. yellow, yellow base, amber windows ..$14 – 18
  5. yellow with yellow base, green windows ..$14 – 18

Camping Cruiser Motor Coach, 4⅜", King Size K-27, 1971
  1. yellow with orange roof ....$14 – 18

Cargo Hauler, 8¾", King Size K-33, 1978
  1. blue, "Gauntlet" ....$20 – 30
  2. blue, "US Steel" ....$20 – 30
  3. yellow, "Gauntlet" ....$30 – 50
  4. yellow, "K" ....$20 – 30
  5. yellow, "MW" ....$20 – 30

Cargo Hauler and Pallet Loader, with K-15 Fork Lift, 7½", King Size K-20, 1973 ....$20 – 30

Car Recovery Vehicle, King Size K-2, 1977
  1. green, "Car Recovery" labels, with K-37
    Sand Cat ....$20 – 30
  2. green, "24 Hour" labels, with K-37
    Sand Cat ....$20 – 30
  3. metallic blue, "24 Hour" labels, with K-59
    Ford Capri II ....$20 – 30
  4. tan and white, "Race Haulage" labels, with
    K-60 Cobra Mustang ....$35 – 50
  5. yellow, "im Auftrag des ADAC" labels, with K-48
    Mercedes Benz 350 SLC,
    Germany issue ....$45 – 60

Car Transporter, 10½", King Size K-10, 1976
  1. "4" ....$25 – 40
  2. "Auto Transport" ....$25 – 40
  3. wild horse design ....$30 – 45

Caterpillar Bulldozer, 3⁵⁄₁₆", King Size K-3, 1960 ..$65 – 90

Caterpillar Earth Scraper, 4½", Major Pack M-1, 1957 ....$125 – 175

Caterpillar Traxcavator, 4⅛", King Size K-8, 1970
  1. yellow ....$25 – 40
  2. silver-gray, Mexico issue ....$65 – 90

Caterpillar Traxcavator Road Ripper, 5½", King Size K-42, 1979; Construction CS-1, 1991
  1. yellow with yellow metal shovel, black roof,
    England cast, K-42 ....$18 – 24
  2. yellow with yellow plastic shovel, black roof,
    England cast, K-42 ....$14 – 18

3. yellow with red plastic shovel, red roof, China
cast, CS-1 . . . .$14 – 18

Cement Mixer (see GMC Cement Mixer, Cement Truck)

Cement Truck, 4", King Size K-26, 1980
1. blue with red base, "Hoch & Tief,"
Germany issue . . . .$30 – 50
2. red with red base, "McAlpine" . . . . . .$20 – 30
3. yellow with black base, "McAlpine" . .$14 – 18
4. yellow with red base, "McAlpine" . . . .$18 – 24

Chevelle (see Chevrolet Chevelle)

Chevrolet 3100 Pickup, 1955, 4⅜", Matchbox Collectibles Fabulous Fifties Road Service YRS-04, introduced in 1996; YIS-01, introduced in 1998

1. **"Harley-Davidson Motorcycles," black,
porcelain crates in back, Matchbox
Collectibles YIS-01** . . . .**$30 – 40**
2. "Ray's Dixie Gasoline AAA Service,"
YRS-04 . . . .$30 – 40

Chevrolet 3100 Pickup, 1956, 4½", Matchbox Collectibles Fabulous Fifties Road Service YRS-03, introduced in 1996; YIS-03, introduced in 1998
1. "Chevrolet Motors," "Chevrolet Genuine Parts,"
blue with two porcelain engine blocks
in back, YIS-03 . . . .$30 – 40

2. "Harris Bros. Mobilgas," dark blue with
accessories in back, YRS-03 . . . .$30 – 40

Chevrolet 3100 Pickup, 1957, 4⅜"
1. turquoise with white top, Matchbox
Collectibles '57 Chevys Collection . . . . .$25 – 35

2. **"AA American Ground Service," white,
porcelain luggage in back, YIS-04,
introduced in 1998** . . . .**$30 – 40**

Chevrolet Bel Air, 1955, DYG-16, introduced in 1998; Matchbox Collectibles Oldies but Goodies II, issued 2004
1. red and cream, DYG-16 . . . .$20 – 30
2. red and cream, Oldies but Goodies II . .$9 – 12

Chevrolet Bel Air, 1957, The Dinky Collection DY-2, introduced in 1989; DYG-02, introduced in 1996; Matchbox Collectibles '57 Chevys Collection; Budweiser Sports Cars DYM-37600, introduced in 1999; Oldies but Goodies I, issued 2004
1. black with flames, Matchbox
Collectibles . . . .$12 – 16
2. Boxing, DYM-37600 . . . .$30 – 40
3. metallic lavender with white roof, '57
Chevys Collection . . . .$24 – 36
4. red with white roof, DY-2 . . . .$18 – 24
5. red with white roof, DYG-02 . . . .$18 – 24
6. red with white roof, Oldies But Goodies I . .$9 – 12

Chevrolet Bel Air Convertible, 1957, The Dinky Collection DY-27, introduced in 1991
1. red, Matchbox Collectibles '57 Chevys . .$25 – 40
2. red and yellow, Matchbox Collectibles
Coca-Cola Collection . . . .$12 – 18
3. sky blue with brown and blue interior,
DY-27 . . . .$100 – 150
4. sky blue with cream and blue
interior, DY-27 . . . .$20 – 30

Chevrolet Bel Air Nomad, 1957, Matchbox Collectibles '57 Chevys VCV-01, introduced in 1998

1. black with white roof . . . .**$20 – 30**

Chevrolet Camaro SS396, 1968, Matchbox Collectibles Muscle Cars YMC-06, introduced in 1997
    1. black with red pinstripes, YMC-06 . . . .$30 – 40
    2. black, "Coca-Cola It's Twice Time" . .$30 – 40

Chevrolet Camaro Turbo, 4⅝", Specials SP11/12, 1984; King Size K-10, 1989, Turbo Specials TS1, Muscle Cars, LA Wheels
    1. black with orange and black stripes, chrome
       rims, Muscle Cars . . . .$8 – 10
    2. red, "56," chrome rims, Specials SP12 . .$8 – 10
    3. white, "7 Total," rims without chrome,
       Specials SP12 . . . .$8 – 10
    4. white, "7 Total," rims without chrome,
       Turbo Specials TS1 . . . .$8 – 10
    5. white, "Firestone 4," unchromed rims,
       Turbo Specials TS1 . . . .$8 – 10

6. white, "Goodyear 18," chromed rims,
    Specials SP11 . . . .**$8 – 10**
    7. white, "Michelin 3," chromed rims,
       Specials SP11 . . . .$8 – 10
    8. white, "Michelin 3," unchromed rims,
       LA Wheels, King Size K-10 . . . .$8 – 10
    9. white with orange and black stripes, chromed
       rims, Muscle Cars . . . .$8 – 10
    10. yellow, "7 Total," unchromed rims, LA
       Wheels, King Size K-10 . . . .$8 – 10

Chevrolet Chevelle SS396, 1966, Matchbox Collectibles Muscle Cars YMC-08, introduced in 1998
    1. metallic red . . . .$30 – 40

Chevrolet Chevelle SS454, 1970, Matchbox Collectibles Muscle Cars YMC-01, introduced in 1996
    1. red, no markings . . . .$30 – 40
    2. red, "Mattel Annual Operations
       Meeting 1998" . . . .$800 – 1,000

Chevrolet Corvette, pewter, The Dinky Collection DY-923, introduced in 1992 . . . .$40 – 50

Chevrolet Corvette, 1956, The Dinky Collection DY-23, introduced in 1991; DYG-06, introduced in 1996; Matchbox Collectibles Oldies but Goodies I, issued 2004
    1. black, DYG-06 . . . .$18 – 24
    2. black, Oldies but Goodies I . . . .$9 – 12
    3. metallic copper, DY-23 . . . .$18 – 24
    4. red, DY-23 . . . .$12 – 16

Chevrolet Corvette, 1957
    1. white, Matchbox Collectibles '57
       Chevys . . . .$25 – 40
    2. baby blue with removable hardtop,
       Matchbox Collectibles Corvette
       Collection . . . .$20 – 30

Chevrolet Corvette, 1993 40th Anniversary Edition, burgundy, Matchbox Collectibles Corvette Collection . . . .$20 – 30

Chevrolet Corvette, 1997, red, Matchbox Collectibles Corvette Collection . . . .$20 – 30

Chevrolet Corvette Convertible, 1953, white, Matchbox Collectibles Corvette Collection . . .$20 – 30

Chevrolet Corvette Split Window Stingray, 1963, silver, Matchbox Collectibles Corvette Collection . . . .$20 – 30

Chevrolet Corvette Stingray Convertible, 1969, yellow, Matchbox Collectibles Corvette Collection . . . .$20 – 30

Chevrolet Corvette Caper Cart (see **Corvette Caper Cart**)

Chevrolet Impala, 1959, DYG-09, introduced in 1998; Matchbox Collectibles Oldies but Goodies II, issued 2004
    1. white, DYG-09 . . . .$20 – 30
    2. white, Oldies but Goodies II . . . .$9 – 12

Chevrolet Model AK Half-Ton Pickup, 1941, YTC-01, introduced in 1999

Chevrolet Nomad (see **Chevrolet Bel Air Nomad**)

1. blue, no markings . . . .$30 – 40

1. metallic light gray . . . .$24 – 32

Chevrolet Pickup, 1955, 1:43 scale, 4½"
1. "Budweiser," red and white, Matchbox Collectibles YVT-04, introduced in 1999 . .$30 – 40
2. "Chevrolet General Parts & Service," Matchbox Collectibles American Giants Collection . . . .$30 – 40
3. "Fred's Service," "Emergency AAA," red with accessories in back, Matchbox Collectibles Road Service YRS-01, introduced in 1996 . . . .$30 – 40
4. "Harley Davidson," Matchbox Collectibles American Giants Collection . . . .$30 – 40
5. red with porcelain Christmas tree, Matchbox Collectibles Santa Claus Collection YSC-02, introduced in 1996 . . . .$50 – 70

Chevrolet Pickup, 1957, 1:43 scale, 4½"
1. "American Airlines," Matchbox Collectibles American Giants Collection . . . .$30 – 40
2. "The Coca-Cola Bottling Company... It's The Real Thing," "Atlanta Bottling Co.," red, YPC-02, introduced in 1998 . . . .$30 – 40

Chieftain Tank, 4¾", Battle Kings BK-103, 1974 .$35 – 50

Chrysler Town and Country, 1947, DYG-10, introduced in 1998; Matchbox Collectibles Oldies but Goodies II, issued 2004
1. tan with woodtone sides, DYG-10 . . . .$20 – 30
2. tan with woodtone sides, Oldies but Goodies II . . . .$9 – 12

Churchill Mk. IV, Matchbox Collectibles Great Tanks of World War II DYM-37584, issued 2000 .$30 – 40

Citroen 15CV, 1952, The Dinky Collection DY-22, introduced in 1991
1. black . . . .$12 – 16
2. cream . . . .$12 – 16

Citroen 2CV, 1949, VEM-03, introduced in 1997

Citroen 2CV, 1957, The Dinky Collection DY-32, introduced in 1992; Exclusive Editions DYM-36840, introduced in 1999
1. gray, DY-32 . . . .$18 – 24
2. yellow and black, DYM-36840 . . . .$40 – 50

Citroen H-Type Van, 1947, Matchbox Collectibles "Taste of France" Collection, introduced in 1993
1. "Brie Marcillat," cream, YTF-04 . . . .$18 – 24
2. "Brisbane International Motor Show," metallic gray with maroon roof . . . .$60 – 80
3. "Champagne Taittinger," metallic gray with maroon roof, YTF-05 . . . .$18 – 24
4. "Evian," pink, YTF-01 . . . .$18 – 24
5. "Martell Cordon Bleu," cream and dark blue, YTF-02 . . . .$18 – 24
6. "Moutarde de Meaux Pommery," cream with red roof, YTF-06 . . . .$18 – 24
7. "Yoplait," white and lime green, YTF-03 $18 – 24

Citroen SM, 4½", King Size K-33, 1972 . . . . . .$14 – 18

Citroen SM Doctor's Emergency Car, 4½", King Size K-62, 1977 . . . .$14 – 18

Claas Matador Combine Harvester, 5½", King Size K-9, 1967

1. green with no driver, green and white "Claas" label . . . .**$40 – 60**
2. green with white driver, green and white "Claas" decal . . . .$40 – 60
3. green with white driver, green and white "Claas" label . . . .$40 – 60
4. red with tan driver, green and white "Claas" label . . . .$60 – 80
5. red with tan driver, red and white "Claas" decal . . . .$40 – 60
6. red with no driver, red and white "Claas" decal . . . .$40 – 60

Cobra Mustang (see **Ford Cobra Mustang**)

Command Force - set of four vehicles, Adventure 2000 K-2005, 1977 . . . .$65 – 90
Includes:
'68, Cosmobile, 3"
#59 Planet Scout, 3"
#2 Hovercraft, 3"
K-2004 Rocket Striker, 4⅜"

Commer 8-CWT Van, 1948, The Dinky Collection DY-8, introduced in 1989
1. "His Master's Voice," dark blue . . . .$12 – 16
2. "Sharp's Toffee," red . . . .$12 – 16

Construction Transporter, 6⅜", King Size K-36, 1978
1. with #26 Site Dumper and #29 Tractor Shovel . . . .$20 – 30
2. with #26 Site Dumper and #48 Sambron Jacklift . . . .$20 – 30
3. with Super Kings Mercury, lime green . .$25 – 40

Container Truck (see **Scammell Container Truck**)

Cooper-Jarrett Interstate Double Freighter with Hendrickson Relay Tractor, 11⅛", Major Pack M-9, 1962
1. gray trailers . . . .$175 – 225

2. silver trailers . . . .**$175 – 225**

Cord 812, 1937, Models of Yesteryear Y-18, introduced in 1979; Matchbox Collectibles Cars of the Rich & Infamous DYM-35178, introduced in 1999
1. dark blue, DYM35178 . . . .$30 – 40
2. metallic red with white roof, silver disc wheels, Y-18 . . . .$18 – 24
3. metallic red with white roof, silver spoked wheels, Y-18 . . . .$20 – 30
4. plum with white roof, chrome spoked wheels, Y-18 . . . .$30 – 40
5. yellow with tan roof, chrome spoked wheels, Y-18 . . . .$20 – 30

Corvette Caper Cart, 4¼", King Size K-55, 1975
1. dark blue . . . .$14 – 18
2. light blue . . . .$18 – 24
3. metallic orange . . . .$14 – 18

Corvette Power Boat Set, 10⅛", King Size K-58, 1975 (K-55 Corvette Caper Cart with K-25 Seaburst Power Boat and Trailer) . . . .$30 – 40

Crane Truck (see **Mobile Crane, Military Crane Truck**)

Crescent Limited Locomotive and Coal Tender on wooden stand with two track sections, YSL-001, introduced in 1994 (made by Mantua) $200 – 250

Crossley, 1918, Models of Yesteryear Y-13, introduced in 1973

1. blue-gray with tan roof and canopy, "RAF" . . . .**$60 – 75**
2. blue-gray with olive roof and canopy, "RAF" . . . .$70 – 85
3. blue-gray with black roof and canopy, "RAF" . . . .$275 – 325
4. cream with green roof and canopy, "Carlsberg" . . . .$18 – 24

5. dark green with cream roof and canopy, "Waring's" . . . .**$20 – 30**
6. gold plated with black roof and canopy, cross labels . . . .$50 – 60
7. gold plated with black roof and coal load, "Coal and Coke" . . . .$50 – 60
8. red with black roof and coal load, "Coal and Coke" . . . .$18 – 24
9. yellow with black roof and coal load, "Kohle & Koks" . . . .$18 – 24

Crossley Beer Lorry, 1918, Models of Yesteryear Y-26, introduced in 1984
1. "Gonzales Byass," white with maroon canopy . . . .$18 – 24

2. "Lowenbrau," light blue with tan canopy, brown barrels . . . .**$18 – 24**
3. "Romford Brewery," black with black canopy, dark brown barrels . . . .$18 – 24

Crusader Tank, 4⅜", Adventure 2000 K-2003, 1977 . . . .$40 – 65

Cuda 440 6-Pack, 1971 (see **Plymouth Cuda 440 6-Pack**)

Curtiss-Wright Rear Dumper, 5¾", King Size K-7, 1961 . . . .$100 – 125

DAF 3300 Space Cab, 7¾" tractor tanker trailer, Matchbox Collectibles Official Gas Tankers Collection

1. "British Petroleum" . . . .$18 – 24

DAF Aircraft Transporter, King Size K-128, 1986
1. red, light brown jet plane, Macau cast .$16 – 20
2. red, metallic gray airplane with red pontoons, China cast, Great Britain issue . . . . . .$40 – 60

DAF Ambulance, 3¾", Battle Kings BK-112, 1977 . .$40 – 65

DAF Car Transporter, 9", King Size K-11, 1969
1. metallic blue with gold trailer, black plastic tires . . . .$90 – 120
2. yellow with yellow and orange trailer, black plastic tires . . . .$55 – 75
3. yellow with yellow and red trailer, Superfast wheels . . . .$30 – 50
4. yellow with yellow and orange trailer, Superfast wheels . . . .$30 – 50

DAF Helicopter Transporter, King Size K-126, 1986; Emergency EM-9, 1991
1. "Coast Guard," white, EM-9 . . . .$18 – 24
2. "Royal Navy," blue, K-126 . . . .$18 – 24

Daimler, 1911, Models of Yesteryear Y-13, introduced in 1966; Medallion Series YMS-05, introduced in 1996
1. blue . . . .$20 – 30
2. gold plated . . . .$50 – 60

3. maroon with gold pinstripe trim, YMS-05 . .**$20 – 30**
4. silver plated . . . .$50 – 60

5. yellow . . . .**$30 – 40**

Datsun 260Z Rally Car, 4⅛", King Size K-52, 1974
    1. yellow . . . .$14 – 18
    2. metallic gray . . . .$14 – 18
    3. green (from K-76 Volvo Rally Set) . . . . .$14 – 18

Delahaye 145, 1946, The Dinky Collection DY-14, introduced in 1990
    1. metallic dark blue . . . .$12 – 16
    2. metallic red . . . .$12 – 16

DeSoto, 1948, DYG-14, introduced in 1998
    1. burgundy, DYG-14 . . . .$20 – 30
    2. burgundy, Matchbox Collectibles Oldies
       but Goodies II . . . .$9 – 12

Diamond T, 1933, YVT-01, introduced in 1999
    1. "Budweiser - King of Bottled Beers," red and
       white, YVT-01, introduced in 1999 . . .$30 – 40

Diamond T, 1948, Matchbox Collectibles Big Rig
    Cabs DYM35216, introduced in 1999 . . .$40 – 50

Diddler Trolley Bus, 1931, Models of Yesteryear Y-10, introduced in 1988; Matchbox Collectibles European Transports YET-03, introduced in 1996
    1. "Ronuk," "Jeyes' Kills," red, Y-10 . . . . .$30 – 40

    2. "Lion Black Lead," red, YET-03 . . . . . .$24 – 32

Diesel Road Roller, 3¼", King Size K-9, 1962
    1. green with gray driver . . . .$90 – 120
    2. green with red driver . . . .$60 – 80

Digger and Plow, 5⅛", King Size K-25, 1977, Construction CS-7, 1991
    1. red . . . .$25 – 40
    2. orange . . . .$20 – 30
    3. yellow . . . .$18 – 24
    4. green, CS-7 . . . .$18 – 24

Digger and Plow Transporter (see Peterbilt Digger and Plow Transporter)

Dinkum Dumper, 4¼", Major Pack M-10-A, 1962
    1. black plastic tires on silver metal rims . .$85 – 100
    2. black plastic tires on red plastic rims . .$85 – 100

Doctor's Emergency Car (see Citroen SM Doctor's Emergency Car)

Dodge Airflow Van, 1937
    1. red and white, "Anheuser-Busch Budweiser
       Everywhere". YVT-02, introduced
       in 1999 . . . .$30 – 40
    2. yellow and red, "Coca-Cola," Matchbox
       Collectibles Coca-Cola Collection . .$12 – 18

    3. yellow and green, "Zephyr," Great Beers of the
       World . . . .$12 – 18

Dodge Ambulance, 5⁵⁄₁₆", K-38, 1980
    1. "Ambulance" . . . .$18 – 24
    2. "Notarzt," Germany issue . . . .$30 – 50

Dodge Articulated Horse Box, 6½", King Size K-18, 1966
    1. red cab, unpainted base, tan horse box,
       black plastic tires . . . .$60 – 80

    2. red cab, gray base, tan horse box, black
       plastic tires . . . .$30 – 50

Dodge Challenger R/T, 1971, Matchbox Collectibles Muscle Cars YMC-02, introduced in 1998
    1. purple . . . .$30 – 40

Dodge Charger, 4½", King Size K-22, 1969
   1. dark blue . . . .$60 – 80

Dodge Chatrorger, 1969, Matchbox Collectibles Muscle Cars YMC-10, induced in 1998; Budweiser Sports Cars DYM-37598, introduced in 1999; VCV01-M, introduced in 2000

   1. orange-red, VCV01-M . . . .**$30 – 40**
   2. orange-red, YMC-10 . . . .$30 – 40
   3. Racing, DYM-37598 . . . .$30 – 40

Dodge Custom Van, 5⁵⁄₁₆", King Size K-80, 1980 .$14 – 18

Dodge Delivery Van, 5⁵⁄₁₆", King Size K-11, 1981
   1. blue, "Frankfurter Allgemeine,"
      Germany issue . . . .$40 – 60
   2. blue, "Suchard Express," France issue .$40 – 60
   3. yellow, "Michelin" . . . .$15 – 20
   4. yellow, "Suchard Express," France issue . .$60 – 80

Dodge Dragster, 4½", King Size K-22, 1971
   1. orange, "Bender" . . . .$18 – 24
   2. orange, "Dinamite" . . . .$20 – 30
   3. pink . . . .$12 – 18 (see **Drag Pack**)
   4. purple . . . .$12 – 18 (see **Drag Pack**)

Dodge Monaco and Travel Trailer, 8¼", King Size
   K-68, 1979 . . . .$16 – 20

Dodge Monaco Fire Chief, 4½", King Size K-67, 1978

   1. yellow, "Hackensack" . . . .**$18 – 24**
   2. red, "Fire Chief" . . . .$18 – 24

Dodge Power Wagon, 1946, YTC-02, introduced in 1999
   1. dark green, no markings . . . .$30 – 40

   2. red, no markings . . . .$30 – 40

Dodge Routemaster, Matchbox Collectibles "Power of the Press" YPP-04, introduced in 1995

   1. "The New York Times" . . . .**$20 – 30**
   2. "Express Delivery" . . . .$50 – 70

Dodge Route Van Canteen, Matchbox Collectibles Fire Engine Collection YFE-16
   1. red, "Springfield Fire Brigade Auxiliary" . .$35 – 50

Dodge Tractor with Twin Tippers, 11⅞", King Size K-16, 1966
   1. green with yellow dump trailers, black tires
      on red hubs . . . .$150 – 200
   2. yellow with pale blue dump trailers,
      Superfast wheels . . . .$90 – 120

Drag Pack, 11", King Size K-28, 1971
   1. lime green Mercury Commuter, pink
      K-22 Dodge Dragster . . . .$25 – 40
   2. lime green Mercury Commuter, purple
      K-22 Dodge Dragster . . . .$25 – 40
   3. metallic green Mercury Commuter, pink
      K-22 Dodge Dragster . . . .$25 – 40
   4. metallic green Mercury Commuter, purple
      K-22 Dodge Dragster . . . .$25 – 40

Duesenberg Model J Town Car, 1930, Models of Yesteryear Y-4, introduced in 1976; Matchbox Collectibles Cars of the Rich & Infamous DYM35182, introduced in 1999
    1. red, DYM35182 . . . .$30 – 40

    2. brown and beige . . . .**$18 – 24**
    3. light blue . . . .$18 – 24

    4. metallic red with black roof . . . .**$20 – 30**
    5. silver and blue, China cast . . . .$30 – 40
    6. silver and blue, Macau cast . . . .$18 – 24
    7. two-tone green with green roof . . . . .$20 – 30
    8. white with yellow roof . . . .$1,800 – 2,400

Duke of Connaught Locomotive, 1903, Models of Yesteryear Y-14, introduced in 1959 . . . .$70 – 85

Dump Truck (also see **Tipper Truck**)

Dyson Low Loader with Bulldozer (see **Ford Tractor with Dyson Low Loader and Case Tractor Bulldozer**)

Easy Rider Motorcycle, 4¾", King Size K-47, 1973
    1. light brown driver . . . .$14 – 18
    2. orange driver . . . .$14 – 18
    3. white driver . . . .$60 – 80

Emergency Set, Emergency EM-50, 1991 . . .$45 – 50
    Includes:
        Snorkel Fire Engine
        Fire Spotter Plane
        BMW 730 Police
        Helicopter
        Ford Transit Ambulance
        plus accessories

Emergency Van (see **Bedford Emergency Van**)

E.R.A. Remus, 1936, Models of Yesteryear Y-14, introduced in 1986
    1. black with chrome plated wheels . . . .$18 – 24
    2. blue with yellow wheels, England cast .$14 – 18
    3. blue with yellow wheels, China cast . .$30 – 40

ERF Simon Snorkel Fire Engine, 8¼", K-39, 1980; Emergency EM-10, 1991

    1. K-39 . . . .$20 – 30
    2. EM-10 . . . .$14 – 18

Europa Caravelle Caravan (see **Jaguar and Europa Caravelle Caravan, Volvo and Europa Caravelle Caravan**)

Farm Unimog and Livestock Trailer (see **Mercedes Benz Farm Unimog and Livestock Trailer**)

Ferrari 512 BB (Berlinetta Boxer), 4¹¹⁄₁₆", Specials SP3/4, 1984; Super Kings K-3/K-4, 1989; also issued as Super GT Sports, Turbo Specials, Muscle Cars, Alarm Cars, Graffic Traffic, LA Wheels

1. black, "Michelin 88," Specials SP4 . . . . . $8 – 10
2. blue, "Pioneer 11," Specials SP3 . . . . $8 – 10
3. lime green, "Michelin 88," LA Wheels . . $8 – 10
4. orange, "147," Specials SP3 . . . . $8 – 10
5. red, "European University 11," Specials SP4 . $8 – 10
6. white, "147," LA Wheels . . . . $8 – 10
7. white, "Pioneer 11," Turbo Specials TS6 . . $10 – 12
8. white, no markings, Graffic Traffic . . . . $14 – 18
9. white and black, pink flames, "512" . . . . $7 – 9

Ferrari Dino 246/V12, 1957, Models of Yesteryear
Y-16, introduced in 1986 . . . . $18 – 24

Ferrari Dino 246 GTS, 1973, The Dinky Collection DY-
24, introduced in 1991; DY-922, introduced in 1992
1. red, DY-24 . . . . $18 – 24
2. pewter, DY-922 . . . . $40 – 50

Ferrari F40, 4⁵⁄₁₆", King Size K-8/K-9, 1989
1. lime green with clear windows, Matchbox
Preschool / Live 'N Learn . . . . $8 – 10
2. red with black windows, Alarm Car . . . $8 – 10
3. red with clear windows, King Size
K-8, 1989 . . . . $14 – 18
4. white with amber windows,
Graffic Traffic . . . . $14 – 18
5. white with black windows, Alarm Car . . $8 – 10
6. Racer, King Size K-9 . . . . $14 – 18

Ferrari Testarossa, King Size K-149, 1988
1. red, China cast . . . . $8 – 10
2. red, Macau cast . . . . $8 – 10
3. red with detail trim, Ultra Class,
China cast . . . . $16 – 20

Ferrari Testarossa Rally, King Size K-155, 1988
1. yellow . . . . $8 – 10

Fiat 500, 1966, VEM-06, introduced in 1997
1. light green . . . . $24 – 32

Fire Chief's Car (see **Blaze Trailer Fire Chief's Car**)

Fire Control Range Rover, 4⅛", King Size K-64, 1978
1. "Fire Control" . . . . $14 – 18
2. "Falck Zonen," Switzerland issue . . . . . $50 – 70

Fire Engine (see **Magirus Deutz Fire Engine, Iveco Fire
Engine**)

Fire Rescue Set - Unimog and Magirus Deutz Fire
Engine, King Size K-119, 1985; King Size K-138 with
roof lights on fire engine that steer front
wheels, 1986 . . . . $30 – 40

Fire Spotter Airplane Transporter, King Size K-112,
1985; K-134, 1986; Emergency EM-11, 1991

1. K-112 . . . . $20 – 30

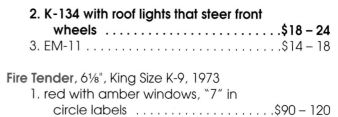

**2. K-134 with roof lights that steer front
wheels** . . . . **$18 – 24**
3. EM-11 . . . . $14 – 18

Fire Tender, 6⅛", King Size K-9, 1973
1. red with amber windows, "7" in
circle labels . . . . $90 – 120
2. red with amber windows, "Fire" labels . . $18 – 24

3. red with clear windows, "Fire" labels   .$18 – 24

Flight Hunter, 4¹³⁄₁₆", Adventure 2000
K-2002, 1977 . . . . $40 – 65

Foden Breakdown Truck, 4¾", King Size K-12, 1963
1. green with silver metal hubs, no cast
roof lights . . . . $70 – 90

**2. green with red plastic hubs, no cast
roof lights** . . . . **$70 – 90**

3. green with red plastic hubs, cast
      roof lights . . . .$70 – 90

Foden Coal Truck, Matchbox Collectibles
Steam-Powered Vehicles Collection . . . .$24 – 32

Foden Ready-Mix Concrete Truck, 4½", King Size K-
13, 1963
   1. orange, "Ready-Mix," black plastic tires on
      silver metal hubs . . . .$70 – 90

2. orange, "Ready-Mix," black plastic tires on
      red plastic hubs . . . .$70 – 90
   3. orange, "RMC," black plastic tires on red
      plastic hubs . . . .$70 – 90

Foden Steam Wagon, 1922, Models of Yesteryear Y-27,
introduced in 1985; Matchbox Collectibles Age of
Steam YAS-12, introduced in 1997
   1. "F. Parker & Co.," rust brown,
      Matchbox Collectibles . . . .$90 – 120
   2. "Frasers," dark green with trailer . . . . .$30 – 40
   3. "Guiness," dark blue . . . .$18 – 24
   4. "Hovis," brown . . . .$18 – 24
   5. "Joseph Rank," dark green . . . .$18 – 24
   6. "McMullen," black . . . .$18 – 24
   7. "Pickfords," blue, no tow hook . . . . . .$18 – 24
   8. "Pickfords," blue, with tow hook . . . . .$30 – 40
   9. "R. Brett & Sons," gray, YAS-12 . . . . . .$30 – 40
   10. "Spillers," cream . . . .$18 – 24
   11. "Tate & Lyle," light brown . . . .$18 – 24

Foden Steam Wagon, 1927, Matchbox Collectibles
"Great Beers of the World" Collection YGB-11, introduced in 1994
   1. "Whitbread's Ale & Stout" . . . .$18 – 24

Foden Tipper Truck, 4¼", King Size K-5, 1961
   1. black plastic tires on silver metal
      wheels . . . .$70 – 95

2. black plastic tires on red plastic
      wheels . . . .$65 – 90

Fokker DR-1 Bi-Plane, Matchbox Collectibles,
   2004 . . . .$16 – 24

Ford AA (see **Ford Model AA**)

Ford Aeromax, 7" tractor-trailer, Matchbox Collectibles North American Brewmasters Collection
   1. "Red Dog" . . . .$16 – 20

Ford Aeromax, 7¾" tractor tanker trailer, Matchbox
Collectibles Official Gas Tankers Collection
   1. "Sunoco" . . . .$25 – 35

Ford Aeromax Box Truck, Matchbox Collectibles
Exclusive Editions DYM-36097, introduced in 1999
   1. "Jack Daniel's," DYM-36097 . . . .$40 – 50

Ford Bronco, 1969, Ford 100th Anniversary Series,
1:43, introduced in 2003

1. orange red with white roof . . . .$16 – 20

Ford Capri Mk 2, 4⅛", King Size K-59, 1976
   1. beige with black roof, red interior . . . .$14 – 18
   2. beige with brown roof, red interior . . .$14 – 18
   3. metallic silver with metallic silver roof,
      white interior . . . .$18 – 24
   4. white with black roof, red interior . . . .$14 – 18
   5. white with white roof, red interior . . . .$16 – 20

Ford Cobra Mustang (see **Ford Mustang Cobra**)

Ford Delivery Van, 4⁵⁄₁₆", King Size K-29, 1978
   1. blue cab, "Elefanten Junge Mode,"
      Germany issue . . . .$35 – 50
   2. blue cab, "Jelly Babies" . . . .$35 – 50
   3. blue cab, "TAA," UK issue . . . .$35 – 50

   4. orange and white cab, "U-Haul" . . . . .$18 – 24
   5. orange cab, "U-Haul" . . . .$20 – 30
   6. red cab, "Avis" . . . .$18 – 24
   7. red cab, "TAA," UK issue . . . .$40 – 60
   8. turquoise cab, "75 Express" . . . .$35 – 50
   9. white cab, "Avis" . . . .$40 – 60
   10. white cab, dark green chassis, "Mr. Softy,"
      Germany issue . . . .$35 – 50
   11. white cab, white chassis, "Mr. Softy" .$25 – 40

Ford E83W 10CWT Van, 1950, The Dinky Collection DY-4, introduced in 1989
   1. "Heinz 57 Varieties," yellow-orange . . .$12 – 16
   2. "Radio Times," olive green . . . .$12 – 16

Ford E83W 10CWT Van and Support Trailer, 1950, Matchbox Collectibles Fire Engine Collection YFE-18, introduced in 1997
   1. "Emergency Fire Services," YFE-18 . . . .$35 – 50

Ford F-100 1953, 4½", Matchbox Collectibles Fabulous Fifties Road Service Collection YRS-02, introduced in 1996
   1. "Flying A Tire Service," black with accessories
      in back . . . .$30 – 40

Ford F-100 1954, 5⅛", Matchbox Collectibles Fabulous Fifties Road Service Collection YRS-04, introduced in 1996; YIS-05, introduced in 1998
   1. "Sinclair Snow Plow," YRS-04 . . . .$30 – 40

   **2. "PRR," porcelain rail and accessories in back,
   YIS-05 . . . .$30 – 40**

Ford F-100 1955, 4½", Matchbox Collectibles Fabulous Fifties Road Service Collection YRS-06, introduced in 1996
   1. "Santa Fe Red Crown Gasoline," white, "Route
      US 66" on canopy, YRS-06 . . . .$45 – 60
   2. "Santa Fe Red Crown Gasoline," white, "Route
      US 84" on canopy, YRS-06 . . . .$30 – 40
   3. "County Fire Marshall," red, fire equipment
      and dalmatians in back . . . .$40 – 55
   4. "Peoria Tractor & Equipment Co.," "Caterpillar,"
      porcelain tool box and tires in back,
      Matchbox Collectibles YIS-02 . . . . . .$30 – 40

Ford F-150, 1953, Matchbox Collectibles YIS-06, introduced in 1998
   1. "Genuine Ford Parts," "Factory Service,"
      red . . . .$30 – 40

Ford Fairlane, 1956, DYG-12, introduced in 1998; Matchbox Collectibles Oldies but Goodies II, issued 2004
   1. white and blue, DYG-12 . . . .$20 – 30
   2. white and blue, Oldies but Goodies II . .$9 – 12

Ford Fairlane 500XL, 1966, Matchbox Collectibles Muscle Cars YMC-09, introduced in 1998

   1. dark blue . . . .$30 – 40

Ford Fire Truck, 1953, introduced in 1997
1. "Garden City F. D. No. 1," Matchbox Collectibles
   Fire Engine Collection YFE-14 . . . .$35 – 50

Ford LTS Series Tractor and Articulated Tanker, 11½",
King Size K-16, 1974
1. "Aral," blue cab . . . .$50 – 70
2. "BP," white cab . . . .$500 – 650
3. "Chemco," black cab . . . .$20 – 30
4. "Exxon," white cab . . . .$20 – 30
5. "LEP International Transport,"
   metallic red . . . .$500 – 650
6. "Quaker State," green cab,
   Canada issue . . . .$90 – 120
7. "Shell," white cab . . . .$20 – 30
8. "Texaco," green cab, US issue . . . . . .$90 – 120

9. "Texaco," metallic red . . . .**$20 – 30**
10. "Texaco," red cab . . . .$20 – 30
11. "Total," white cab . . . .$50 – 70

Ford Model A Breakdown Truck, 1930, Models of Yesteryear Y-7, introduced in 1984

**1. "Barlow Motor Sales," orange,
   England cast** . . . .**$14 – 18**
2. "Barlow Motor Sales," orange,
   Macau cast . . . .$20 – 30
3. "Shell," yellow . . . .$14 – 18

Ford Model A Fire Chief's Car, YFE-12, Matchbox
   Collectibles Fire Engine Collection, introduced
   in 1996 . . . .$25 – 30

Ford Model A Pickup, 1930, Models of Yesteryear Y-
35, introduced in 1990; YPC-05, introduced in 1998

1. "Coca-Cola," "Atlanta Bottling Company -
   Atlanta, Georgia," ice chest in back . .$30 – 40
2. "From Our Devon Creamery - Ambrosia" . .$18 – 24
3. "W. Clifford & Sons," "Fresh Farm Milk" . .$18 – 24

Ford Model A Van, 1930, Models of Yesteryear Y-22,
introduced in 1982; Matchbox Collectibles "Great
Beers of the World" Collection YGB-01, introduced in
1993; "Power of the Press" YPP-08, introduced in
1995; YWG-01, introduced in 1997; Charity series
YCH-07, introduced in 1998
1. "Ballantine's," dark blue, YWG-01 . . . .$20 – 30
2. "Canada Poste," red with black
   roof, Y-22 . . . .$18 – 24
3. "Castlemaine XXXX," YGB-01 . . . .$18 – 24
4. "Cherry Blossom," white with black roof,
   Macau cast, Y-22 . . . .$18 – 24
5. "Cherry Blossom," white with black roof,
   China cast, Y-22 . . . .$30 – 40
6. "Coca-Cola," yellow and red, Matchbox
   Collectibles Coca-Cola Collection . .$12 – 18
7. "Lyon's Tea," blue with white roof,
   Macau cast, Y-22 . . . .$18 – 24
8. "Lyon's Tea," blue with white roof,
   China cast, Y-22 . . . .$30 – 40
9. "Maggi's," yellow with red roof, Y-22 . .$18 – 24
10. "OXO," red with black roof, Y-22 . . . .$14 – 18
11. "Pratt's," white with black roof, Y-22 . .$18 – 24
12. "Ronald McDonald House," white with
   red roof, YCH-07, Australia issue . . . .$30 – 40
13. "Spratt's," reddish brown with white
   roof, Y-22 . . . .$18 – 24
14. "The Washington Post," YPP-08 . . . . .$18 – 24

15. "Toblerone," beige with red roof, Y-22 . .$18 – 24
16. "Walter's Palm Toffee," cream with
   red roof, Y-22 . . . .$18 – 24

Ford Model A Woody Wagon, 1929, Models of Yesteryear Y-21, introduced in 1981
1. "A&J Box," metallic bronze and brown . .$18 – 24
2. "A&J Box," rust and brown . . . .$18 – 24
3. "Carter's Seeds, blue and cream . . . .$18 – 24

4. yellow and brown . . . .$20 – 30

Ford Model AA 1½ Ton Pickup Truck, 1932, Models of Yesteryear Y-62, introduced in 1992; Matchbox Collectibles "Great Beers of the World" Collection YGB-05, introduced in 1993; YGB-16, introduced in 1995; YGB-20, introduced in 1996; Matchbox Collectibles "Power of the Press" YPP-05, introduced in 1995; Matchbox Collectibles Santa Claus Collection YSC-03, introduced in 1996; YPC-06, introduced in 1998
    1. "Carlsberg Pilsner," YGB-05 . . . .$18 – 24
    2. "Corona Extra," YGB-16 . . . .$18 – 24
    3. "Delicious, Refreshing Coca-Cola," yellow
       and red, cases in back . . . .$30 – 40
    4. "G. W. Peacock," Y-62 . . . .$25 – 40
    5. "Happy Holidays from Clayton Feed & Grain,"
       Matchbox Collectibles . . . .$30 – 50

6. "Los Angeles Times," YPP-05 . . . .$20 – 30
7. "Stroh's Beer," YGB-20 . . . .$18 – 24
8. "Teacher's," brown, YWG-06 . . . .$20 – 30

Ford Model AA Fire Engine, 1932, YFE-06, Matchbox Collectibles Fire Engine Collection, introduced in 1995; YFE-28, introduced in 1999; Matchbox Collectibles Santa Claus Collection YSC-04, introduced in 1997
    1. red, no markings, YFE-06 . . . .$25 – 30
    2. red, "Clayton Fire Brigade," Santa and Mrs.
       Claus in back with presents, YSC-04 .$50 – 65
    3. green, "White Mountain National Forest,"
       "Prevent Forest Fires," YFE-29 . . . .$40 – 55

Ford Model AA Open Fire Engine, YFE-09, Matchbox Collectibles Fire Engine Collection, introduced in 1996; Matchbox Collectibles Santa Claus Collection YSC-03, introduced in 1997
    1. red, no markings, YFE-09 . . . .$25 – 30
    2. red with porcelain Santa in back, YSC-03. .$60 – 80

Ford Model T, 1911, Models of Yesteryear Y-1, introduced in 1965; Matchbox Collectibles Medallion Series YMS-01, introduced in 1996
    1. black with black seats, black roof, Y-1 . .$375 – 450
    2. black with tan seats, black roof, Y-1 . .$20 – 30
    3. black with gold pinstripes, brown seats,
       black roof, YMS-01 . . . .$20 – 30

4. cream, Y-1 . . . .$20 – 30

5. red, Y-1 . . . .$20 – 30
6. silver plated, Y-1 . . . .$50 – 60
7. white, Y-1 . . . .$30 – 40

Ford Model T Fire Engine, 1916, 4¾", Matchbox Collectibles Fire Engine Collection YFE-22 .$35 – 50

Ford Model T Tanker, 1912, Models of Yesteryear Y-3, introduced in 1982
    1. "BP," dark green with red tank, white roof, gold spoked wheels . . . .$40 – 60
    2. "BP," dark green with red tank, white roof, red spoked wheels . . . .$12 – 18
    3. "Carnation Farm Products," cream with maroon tank, white roof . . . .$18 – 24
    4. "Castrol," dark green with dark green tank, white roof, gold spoked wheels . . . .$18 – 24
    5. "Castrol," dark green with dark green tank, white roof, red spoked wheels . . . . .$30 – 35

    6. "Express Dairy," blue with blue tank, white roof, gold spoked wheels . . . .$18 – 24
    7. "Express Dairy," blue with blue tank, white roof, red spoked wheels . . . .$30 – 35
    8. "Mobiloil," blue and red with blue tank and roof, red 12-spoke wheels . . . .$18 – 24
    9. "Mobiloil," blue and red with blue tank and roof, red 24-spoke wheels . . . .$30 – 40
    10. "Red Crown Gasoline," red with red tank and roof . . . .$20 – 30
    11. "Shell," yellow with yellow tank, white roof . . . .$18 – 24
    12. "Zerolene," green with white tank, white roof, gold spoked wheels . . . .$90 – 120

Ford Model T Truck, 1912 (see **Ford Model T Van, 1912**)

Ford Model T Van, 1912, Models of Yesteryear Y-12, introduced in 1979; Matchbox Collectibles "Great Beers of the World" Collection YGB-14, introduced in 1995; Matchbox Collectibles "Great Beers of the World" Collection YGB-19, introduced in 1996; Matchbox Collectibles Charity Series YCH-01, introduced in 1995; YWG-05, introduced in 1997; YPC-04, introduced in 1998
    1. "25th Anniversary," green with gray roof, yellow wheels . . . .$18 – 24
    2. "Arnott's Biscuits," red with black roof, gold wheels . . . .$175 – 225
    3. "Bang & Olufsen," white and maroon with

black roof, red wheels . . . .$275 – 325
    4. "Bird's Custard," blue with yellow roof, red wheels . . . .$18 – 24
    5. "Cada Toys," yellow with black roof, red wheels . . . .$275 – 325
    6. "Camberley News," yellow with black roof, red wheels . . . .$275 – 325

    7. "Enjoy Coca-Cola," cream with black roof, red wheels . . . .$40 – 60
    8. "Coca-Cola," cream with black roof, silver wheels . . . .$60 – 75
    9. "Coleman's Mustard," yellow with black roof, red wheels . . . .$18 – 24
    10. "Coleman's Mustard," yellow with black roof, silver wheels . . . .$30 – 40
    11. "Deans for Toys," yellow with black roof, red wheels . . . .$275 – 325
    12. "Harrods," dark green with beige roof, gold wheels . . . .$18 – 24
    13. "Ice Cold Coca-Cola Sold Here," red and yellow . . . .$30 – 40
    14. "Kirin Lager," YGB-14 . . . .$18 – 24
    15. "Model Collectors Extravaganza" yellow with black roof, red wheels . . . .$275 – 325

    16. "Pepsi-Cola," white with red roof, blue fenders . . . .$18 – 24
    17. "Ronald McDonald House," YCH-01, Australia issue . . . .$150 – 200

18. "Sheep Dip, The Original Oldbury,"
    olive green, YWG-05 . . . .$20 – 30
19. "Smith's Crisps," blue with white roof,
    red wheels . . . .$18 – 24
20. "Suze," yellow with black roof,
    red wheels . . . .$18 – 24
21. "Suze," yellow with black roof,
    silver wheels . . . .$30 – 40
22. "Yuengling's, YGB-19 . . . .$18 – 24

Ford Model TT Van, 1926, Models of Yesteryear Y-21, introduced in 1989; Matchbox Collectibles Y-39, introduced in 1996; Matchbox Collectibles "Great Beers of the World" Collection YGB-02, introduced in 1993; YGB-13, introduced in 1995; YWG-02, introduced in 1997; YVT-03, introduced in 1999.

1. "3rd MICA Convention Sydney" . . . .$90 – 120
2. "Anchor Steam Beer," YGB-13 . . . . . .$18 – 24
3. "Anheuser-Busch Bottled Beer,"
    black and red, YVT-03 . . . .$30 – 40
4. "Antiques Road Show-Next Generation
    1992," black . . . .$1,750 – 2,000

5. **"Beck & Co.," YGB-02** . . . .**$18 – 24**
6. "Coca-Cola," yellow and red, Matchbox
    Collectibles Coca-Cola Collection . .$12 – 18
7. "Drambuie," black, Y-21 . . . .$18 – 24
8. "Jack Daniel's Old No. 7 Brand," Y-39 . .$40 – 55
9. "Long John," black, YWG-02 . . . .$20 – 30
10. "My Bread," beige, Y-21 . . . .$18 – 24
11. "O for an Osram," green with
    red roof, Y-21 . . . .$18 – 24

Ford Model TT Van YCH-02/1 & Ford Model A Van YCH-02/2, Matchbox Collectibles Charity Series YCH-02,

1. YCH-02/1: "Ronald McDonald Charities of
    Australia," red and yellow; YCH-02/2:
    "Camp Quality," light blue, Australia
    issue, 1996 . . . .$150 – 200
2. YCH-02/1: "Ronald McDonald Charities of
    Australia," red; YCH-02/2: "Camp Quality," two-
    tone blue, Australia issue, 1996 . . .$400 – 600

3. YCH-02/1: "Tyco," red and yellow; YCH-02/2:
    "Matchbox," two-tone blue, Hong Kong
    issue, 1997 . . . .$1,600 – 2,000

Ford Model TT Van 2-vehicle set, issued in Australia, 1989

1. "Pro Hart" and "Lunchtime," dark green; "Jenny
    Kee" and "Waratah," dark blue . .$800 – 1,000

Ford Mustang, 1964, Matchbox Collectibles Budweiser Sports Cars DYM-37619, introduced in 1999

1. Rodeo . . . .$30 – 40

Ford Mustang II, 4¼", King Size K-60, 1976

1. metallic blue . . . .$14 – 18

Ford Mustang Boss 429, 1970, Matchbox Collectibles Muscle Cars YMC-05, introduced in 1997

1. orange, YMC-05 . . . .$30 – 40
2. yellow, "It's The Real Thing,"
    "Coca-Cola" . . . .$30 – 40

Ford Mustang Cobra, 4¼", King Size K-60, 1978

1. enamel red, part of K-2 Car
    Recovery Vehicle . . . .$24 – 32
2. metallic red, part of K-2 Car
    Recovery Vehicle . . . .$24 – 32
3. white . . . .$14 – 18

Ford Mustang Fastback, 1967 (see **Ford Mustang GT 2+2 Fastback Coupe, 1967**)

Ford Mustang GT 2+2 Fastback Coupe, 1967, The Dinky Collection DY-16, introduced in 1990; DYG-01, introduced in 1996; Matchbox Collectibles Oldies but Goodies I, issued 2004

1. dark blue, DYG-01 . . . .$18 – 24
2. dark blue, Matchbox Collectibles Oldies
    but Goodies I . . . .$9 – 12
3. dark green, DY-16 . . . .$12 – 16
4. metallic light green, DY-16 . . . .$18 – 24
5. red, Matchbox Collectibles . . . .$20 – 30
6. white, DY-16 . . . .$18 – 24

Ford Pickup, 1940, YTC-03, introduced in 1999

1. **dark red, YTC-03** . . . .**$30 – 40**
2. red and black, "Budweiser," YVT-05 . .$30 – 40

Ford Pickup, 1953, 1:43 scale, 4½"
    1. "Ford Genuine Parts," Matchbox Collectibles
       American Giants Collection . . . . . .$30 – 40

Ford Pickup, 1954 (see **Ford F-100, 1954**)

Ford Pickup, 1955, 1:43 scale, 4½"
    1. "Caterpillar," Matchbox Collectibles
       American Giants Collection . . . . . .$30 – 40
    2. Matchbox Collectibles Coca-Cola
       Collection, yellow and red . . . .$12 – 18

Ford Sierra RS500 Cosworth, King Size K-162, 1989
    1. black upper, gray lower . . . .$8 – 10
    2. white upper, gray lower . . . .$8 – 10
    3. white upper and lower . . . .$8 – 10
    4. white upper and lower, "Caltex Bond,"
       Australia issue . . . .$30 – 40

Ford Sierra XR4, King Size K-100, 1983 . . . . . .$12 – 16

Ford Sierra XR4 Rally, King Size K-158, 1988
    1. white, "Total" . . . .$20 – 30

Ford Thunderbird Convertible, 1955, The Dinky Collection DY-31, introduced in 1992; DYG-08, introduced in 1996; Matchbox Collectibles Oldies but Goodies I, issued 2004
    1. black, "Americans Prefer Taste,"
       "Coca-Cola" . . . .$30 – 40
    2. red, DY-31 . . . .$18 – 24
    3. turquoise, DYG-08 . . . .$18 – 24
    4. turquoise, Oldies but Goodies I . . . . . .$9 – 12

Ford Tractor Transporter with three tractors, 9", King Size K-20, 1968
    1. blue cab, metallic silver trailer, Superfast
       wheels, three orange tractors,
       Mexico issue . . . .$250 – 300
    2. blue cab, metallic gold trailer, Superfast wheels,
       three orange tractors, Mexico issue . .$250 – 300
    3. blue cab, yellow trailer, Superfast wheels,
       three orange tractors, Mexico issue . .$250 – 300
    4. fluorescent red cab, Superfast wheels,
       three blue tractors . . . .$150 – 200
    5. red cab, metallic silver trailer, Superfast
       wheels, three orange tractors,
       Mexico issue . . . .$250 – 300

6. red cab, red trailer, black plastic tires, three blue tractors . . . .**$150 – 200**

Ford Tractor with Dyson Low Loader and Case Tractor Bulldozer, 11", King Size K-17, 1966
    1. fluorescent red cab, lime green trailer, "Taylor
       Woodrow," Superfast wheels, orange
       and yellow bulldozer . . . .$60 – 80
    2. green cab and trailer, "Laing," black plastic
       tires, red and dark yellow bulldozer . .$110 – 130
    3. green cab and trailer, "Taylor Woodrow,"
       black plastic tires, red and dark
       yellow bulldozer . . . .$110 – 130
    4. lime green cab and trailer, "Taylor Woodrow,"
       Superfast wheels, orange and
       yellow bulldozer . . . .$90 – 110

Ford Transcontinental Double Freighter, 11", King Size K-21, 1979
    1. blue, "Santa Fe" . . . .$25 – 40
    2. blue, "Sunkist" . . . .$40 – 60
    3. green, "Nichts geht uber Barenmarke,"
       Germany issue . . . .$50 – 70
    4. green, "Polara," Germany issue . . . . .$50 – 70
    5. yellow, "Continental" . . . .$25 – 40
    6. yellow, "Danzas" . . . .$50 – 70
    7. yellow, "Weetabix," UK issue . . . . . .$50 – 70

Ford Transit Ambulance, King Size K-169; Emergency EM-7, 1991 . . . .$9 – 12

Ford Transit Van, King Size K-167, 1989; Construction CS-2, 1991
    1. lavender, "Milka" . . . .$14 – 18
    2. light blue, "Surf N Sun" . . . .$9 – 12
    3. light orange, "Miller Construction," CS-2 . .$9 – 12

Ford U-Haul Truck (see **Ford Delivery Van**)

Ford V-8 Pilot, 1949, The Dinky Collection DY-5, introduced in 1989
    1. black . . . .$12 – 16
    2. metallic gray with black roof . . . .$12 – 16
    3. tan with black roof . . . .$12 – 16

Fordson Tractor and Farm Trailer, 6¼", King Size K-11, 1963
    1. blue with blue steering wheel, plastic tires on
       orange plastic hubs . . . .$65 – 85
    2. blue with blue steering wheel, plastic tires on
       red plastic hubs . . . .$65 – 85
    3. blue with silver steering wheel, plastic tires on
       orange metal hubs . . . .$65 – 85
    4. blue with silver steering wheel, plastic tires on
       orange plastic hubs . . . .$65 – 85

Forestry Range Rover and Trailer, King Size K-89, 1982 . . . .$18 – 24

Forestry Unimog and Trailer, King Size K-98, 1979 . . . .$40 – 60

Fowler B6 Showman's Engine, Models of Yesteryear Y-19, introduced in 1986; Matchbox Collectibles Age of Steam YAS05, introduced in 1996
 1. maroon, "John Hoadley's Mammoth Fair" . . . .$20 – 30

Fowler B6 Showman's Engine with Crane, Matchbox Collectibles Age of Steam YAS-07, introduced in 1997
 1. black, "John Hoadley's Mammoth Fair," "Marstons Road Services Ltd." . . . . . .$25 – 35

Fowler Big Lion Showman's Engine, 1924, Models of Yesteryear Y-9, introduced in 1958 . . . .**$80 – 110**

Freightliner Cabover Semi Tractor-Trailer, 11", 1:58, "Beefeater," The Spirit of London . . . .$75 – 90

Freightliner COE, 4½", Matchbox Collectibles Highway Commanders, 1:58 . . . .$35 – 50

Freightliner COE, 12", 1:58, The Spirit of Budweiser . . . .$75 – 90

Freightliner Container Truck, King Size K-187, 1997; K-190, 1996
 1. "Beefeater - The Spirit of London," Matchbox Collectibles K-187 . . . .$60 – 80
 2. "ingle ells ingle ells - Don't forget the J & B," Matchbox Collectibles K-190 . . . . .$120 – 150

Fruehauf Hopper Train (see **GMC Tractor and Fruehauf Hopper Train**)

Fuzz Buggy, 4½", K-41, 1973
 1. white with black base . . . .$14 – 18
 2. white with red base . . . .$18 – 24

Garage Transporter, King Size K-113, 1985 . . .$20 – 30

Garrett Steam Wagon, 1929, Matchbox Collectibles Age of Steam YAS-09, introduced in 1997
 1. "Rainford Potteries Ltd.," dark blue . . .$30 – 45

Garrett Steam Wagon, 1931, Models of Yesteryear Y-37, introduced in 1990; Y-48, introduced in 1996; Matchbox Collectibles "Great Beers of the World" Collection YGB-03, introduced in 1993; YGB-15, introduced in 1995
 1. "Chester Mystery Players," Y-48 . . . . . .$50 – 65
 2. "Chubb's Safe Deposits," Y-37 . . . .$18 – 24
 3. "Flower's Fine Ale," YGB-15 . . . .$18 – 24
 4. "Milkmaid Brand Milk," Y-37 . . . .$18 – 24
 5. "Pickford's Removals & Warehousing," Y-48 . . . .$50 – 65
 6. "The Swan Brewery Ltd.," YGB-03 . . . .$18 – 24

GMC Ambulance, 1937, Matchbox Collectibles Fire Engine Collection YFE-30, introduced in 1999
 1. white . . . .$40 – 55

GMC Cement Mixer, 5¾", King Size K-6, 1971 .$20 – 30

GMC Rescue Vehicle, YFE-10, Matchbox Collectibles Fire Engine Collection, introduced in 1996 .$25 – 30

GMC Tractor and Fruehauf Hopper Train, Major Pack M-4, 1964; King Size K-4, 1967, 11¼"
 1. gray plastic tires on red rims, Major Pack M-4 . . . .$175 – 225

2. black plastic tires on red rims, Major Pack M-4 . . . .**$125 – 175**
 3. gray plastic tires on red rims, King Size K-4 . . . .$200 – 250

4. black plastic tires on red rims, King Size K-4 . . . .**$125 – 175**

GMC Van, 1937, Models of Yesteryear Y-12, introduced in 1988; Matchbox Collectibles "Great Beers of the World" Collection YGB-08, introduced in 1994; Matchbox Collectibles "Power of the Press" YPP-07,

introduced in 1996; YWG-04, introduced in 1997; YPC-02, introduced in 1998
1. "Baxter's," cream . . . .$18 – 24
2. "Drink Coca-Cola Special Delivery,"
"Nine Million Drinks A Day," YPC-02 . .$30 – 40
3. "Goanna," dark blue . . . .$18 – 24

4. **"Goblin," black with black roof . . . . .$18 – 24**
5. "Goblin," black with gray roof . . . . . .$50 – 60
6. "Laphroaig Islay Malt Whisky," white,
YWG-04 . . . .$20 – 30
7. "Steinlager," YGB-08 . . . .$18 – 24
8. "The Australian," YPP-07 . . . .$18 – 24

GMC Van, 1948, YVT-06, introduced in 1999
1. "Budweiser Lager Beer," red, white and
metallic silver . . . .$30 – 40

Gold State Coach (see **Her Majesty Queen Elizabeth II's Gold State Coach**)

Grain Transporter, 11⅞", King Size K-3, 1980
1. red cab, "Kelloggs" . . . .$30 – 40
2. green, "Heidelberger Zement,"
Germany issue . . . .$50 – 75

Grand Prix Mercedes, 1908 (see **Mercedes, 1908 Grand Prix**)

Gran Fury (see **Plymouth Gran Fury**)

Gus's Gulper, 4¼", K-38, 1973
1. pink . . . .$14 – 18
2. white . . . .$175 – 225

Guy Warrior Car Transporter, 8¼", Major Pack M-8, 1964; King Size K-8, 1967
1. blue-green with orange trailer, gray plastic tires on orange rims, Major Pack M-8 . .$100 – 125
2. blue-green with orange trailer, gray plastic tires on orange rims, King Size K-8 . . . . . .$65 – 90
3. blue-green with orange trailer, black plastic tires on orange rims, King Size K-8 . . .$65 – 90
4. blue-green with orange trailer, black plastic tires on red rims, King Size K-8 . . . . . .$65 – 90
5. blue-green with yellow trailer, black plastic tires on red rims, King Size K-8 . . . . .$500 – 600

6. yellow with yellow trailer, black plastic tires on red rims, King Size K-8 . . . .$50 – 75

Gypsy Caravan, Matchbox Collectibles "Historical Series" Collection YHS-01, introduced in 1993 . . . .$60 – 75

Half Track APC (see **M3A1 Half Track APC**)

Harley-Davidson Cafe Racer, #76320, 1993 .$20 – 30

Harley-Davidson Chopper, King Size K-83, 1994
1. black, Harley-Davidson series . . . .$8 – 10
2. blue, Harley-Davidson series . . . .$8 – 10
3. gold plated, Harley-Davidson series . . .$8 – 10
4. metallic red, Harley-Davidson series . . .$8 – 10
5. purple, Harley-Davidson series . . . .$8 – 10
6. red, Harley-Davidson series . . . .$8 – 10

Harley-Davidson Electraglide Motorcycle, 3", Harley-Davidson Series #76246 . . . .$12 – 16

Harley-Davidson Electraglide Motorcycle, Harley-Davidson Series #76300, 1993 . . . .$20 – 30

Harley-Davidson Electraglide Motorcycle and Rider, 4⁵⁄₁₆", King Size K-83, 1981
1. black, "Harley-Davidson," no rider, Harley-Davidson series . . . .$8 – 10
2. black and white, "California Highway Patrol," Harley-Davidson series . . . .$8 – 10

3. black and white, "Kansas Highway Patrol,"
   Harley-Davidson series . . . .$8 – 10
4. cream, "Florida State Trooper,"
   Harley-Davidson series . . . .$8 – 10
5. dark blue, "Harley-Davidson," no rider,
   Harley-Davidson series . . . .$8 – 10
6. dark blue, "Virginia State Police," no rider,
   Harley-Davidson series . . . .$8 – 10
7. gold plated, Harley-Davidson," no rider,
   Harley-Davidson series . . . .$8 – 10
8. purple, "Harley-Davidson," no rider,
   Harley-Davidson series . . . .$8 – 10
9. red, "Harley-Davidson," no rider,
   Harley-Davidson series . . . .$8 – 10
10. white, "MBPD 17," no rider,
    Harley-Davidson series . . . .$8 – 10
11. white, "Police," England cast . . . .$14 – 18
12. white, "Police," Macau cast . . . .$9 – 12

Harley-Davidson Electraglide Motorcycle and Sidecar, 1:10, Harley-Davidson Series #76310, 1993 . .$55 – 65

Harley-Davidson Fat Boy, 1:9, 1995 . . . .$45 – 55

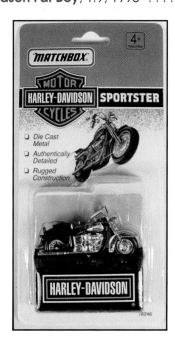

Harley-Davidson Sportster, 3", Harley-Davidson Series #76246 . . . .$20 – 30

Harley-Davidson Sportster, #76330, 1993 . . . .$20 – 30

Harley-Davidson Sportster, King Size K-83, Harley-Davidson series, 1994
1. black . . . .$8 – 10
2. blue . . . .$8 – 10
3. fluorescent yellow . . . .$8 – 10
4. gold plated . . . .$8 – 10
5. purple . . . .$8 – 10
6. red . . . .$8 – 10
7. turquoise . . . .$8 – 10
8. yellow . . . .$8 – 10

Hatra Tractor Shovel, 5⅞", King Size K-3, 1965 . .$60 – 85

Heavy Breakdown Truck, 5⅛", King Size
K-14, 1977 . . . .$16 – 20

Heavy Breakdown Wreck Truck (see **Foden Breakdown Truck**)

Helicopter (also see **Kaman Seasprite Army Helicopter**)

Helicopter, Emergency EM-13, 1991 . . . .$9 – 12

Helicopter Transporter, King Size K-92, 1982 .$20 – 30

Hendrickson Relay Double Freighter (see **Cooper-Jarrett Interstate Double Freighter with Hendrickson Relay Tractor**)

Hercules Mobile Crane, 6⅛", King Size K-12, 1975

1. yellow, "Laing" . . . .$20 – 30
2. two-tone blue, "Hoch & Tief,"
   Germany issue . . . .$50 – 70

Her Majesty Queen Elizabeth II's Gold State Coach, Models of Yesteryear Y-66 Special Limited Edition introduced in 1992 . . . .$40 – 60

Highway Rescue Vehicle, 5⁵⁄₁₆", King Size K-77, 1980
    1. white, "Highway Rescue System" . . . .$14 – 18
    2. white, "Secours Routier," France issue . .$60 – 80
    3. white, "Strassen Service," Germany issue. .$50 – 60

Hispano Suiza, 1938, Models of Yesteryear Y-17, introduced in 1973
    1. green . . . .$20 – 30
       with diorama . . . .$24 – 32

    2. metallic red . . . .**$18 – 24**
    3. two-tone light blue . . . .$18 – 24

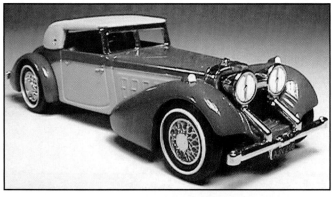

    4. pea green and tan . . . .**$20 – 30**

Holden 50/2106 Utility, 1951, Australia issue, Holden series YHN-03, introduced in 1997; Charity series YCH-11, introduced in 1998
    1. "12th Super Southern Swapmeet Ballarat 2001," lime green with purple canopy, YCH-11 . . . .$30 – 40
    2. "The House that love built... Melbourne Australia," lime green with white canopy, YCH-11 . . . .$30 – 40

    3. khaki tan with removable brown canopy, YHN-03 . . . .$45 – 60

Holden FJ/2104 Panel Van, 1955, Australia issue, Holden series YHN-01, introduced in 1997; Charity series YCH-10, introduced in 1998
    1. "Ronald McDonald House - Sydney Newcastle," pale blue . . . .$30 – 40
    2. beige, "Temora District Ambulance," YHN-01 . . . .$45 – 60
    3. gray, YHN-01 . . . .$45 – 60
    4. yellow, "Automodels Sydney," "Autuomodels Solingen," YHN-01 . . . .$45 – 60

Holden FJ/2106 Utility, 1954, Australia issue, Holden series YHN-02, introduced in 1997
    1. midnight blue with removable black canopy . . . .$45 – 60

Hot Fire Engine, 3⅜", King Size K-53, 1975 . . . .$14 – 18

Hovercraft (see **SRN6 Hovercraft**)

Hoveringham Tipper Truck, 4¼", King Size K-1, 1964

    1. red cab, orange dumper, "Hoveringham" decals . . . .**$60 – 80**
    2. red cab, orange dumper, "Hoveringham" labels . . . .$60 – 80

Hover Raider, 4⅞", Battle Kings BK-105, 1974 .$35 – 50

Howitzer (see **Self Propelled 155mm Howitzer, Troop Carrier with 226mm Howitzer**)

International C Series Pickup, 1934, YTC-06, introduced in 1999
    1. dark purple . . . .$30 – 40

International Tractor (see **McCormick International Tractor**)

Interstate Double Freighter (see **Cooper-Jarrett Interstate Double Freighter with Henderson Relay Tractor**)

Iveco Double Tipper, King Size K-145, 1988 . .$20 – 30

Iveco Fire Engine, Emergency EM-5, 1991 . . .$9 – 12

Iveco Petrol Tanker, King Size K-109, 1984; K-131 with roof lights that steer front wheels, 1986
    1. red, "Texaco," K-131 . . . .$18 – 24
    2. white, "Texaco," K-131 . . . .$18 – 24
    3. yellow, "Shell," K-109 . . . .$9 – 12
    4. yellow, "Shell," K-131 . . . .$9 – 12

Iveco Racing Car Transporter "Ferrari," King Size K-136, 1986 . . . .$20 – 30

Iveco Refuse Truck, King Size K-133, 1986
    1. blue cab, blue container . . . .$60 – 80
    2. blue cab, white container . . . .$90 – 120
    3. maroon cab, maroon container . . . . .$12 – 16

    4. white cab, white container . . . .**$12 – 16**

Iveco Semi Tanker; King Size K-127, 1989
    1. blue cab, "British Farm Produce-Milk" . .$30 – 50

Iveco Skip Truck, King Size K-141, 1987 . . . . . .$9 – 12

Iveco Tanker (see **Iveco Semi Tanker, Iveco Petrol Tanker**)

Iveco Tipper Truck, King Size K-139, 1987; Construction CS-6, 1991

    1. Macau cast, K-139 . . . .**$12 – 16**

    2. China cast, CS-6 . . . .$9 – 12

Jaguar and Europa Caravelle Caravan, 10⅝", King Size K-69, 1980 (also see **Volvo and Europa Caravan**)
    1. blue Jaguar, white caravan . . . .$30 – 40
    2. blue Jaguar, beige caravan . . . .$30 – 40
    3. light brown Jaguar, white caravan . . .$30 – 40
    4. red Jaguar, white caravan . . . .$30 – 40

Jaguar E-Type, pewter, The Dinky Collection DY-921, introduced in 1992 . . . .$40 – 50

Jaguar E-Type Series 1.5 Convertible, top up, 1967, The Dinky Collection DY-1, introduced in 1989
    1. black, black roof . . . .$18 – 21
    2. dark green, black roof . . . .$12 – 16
    3. yellow, black roof . . . .$18 – 21

Jaguar E-Type Series 1.5 Convertible, top down, 1967, The Dinky Collection DY-18, introduced in 1990; Matchbox Collectibles DYB-02, introduced in 1998
    1. black, DY-18 . . . .$18 – 24
    2. red, DY-18 . . . .$12 – 16
    3. red, DYB-02 . . . .$24 – 36

Jaguar SS100, 1936, Models of Yesteryear Y-1, introduced in 1977
    1. cream, England cast . . . .$14 – 18

    2. dark green, England cast . . . .**$14 – 18**
    3. dark yellow with whitewall tires,
        Macau cast . . . .$18 – 24
        with diorama . . . .$20 – 30
    4. light yellow with whitewall tires,
        England cast . . . .$80 – 100
    5. metallic red, China cast . . . .$18 – 24
    6. silver and blue, England cast . . . .$14 – 18

Jaguar SS100, Models of Yesteryear Y-901, introduced in 1991
    1. pewter cast . . . .$80 – 100

Jaguar XJ6, King Size K-146, 1988
    1. dark green . . . .$14 – 18

2. metallic red . . . .**$9 – 12**
3. white, China cast . . . .$8 – 10
4. white, Macau cast . . . .$14 – 18

Jaguar XJ6 Police Car, King Size K-153, 1988;
Emergency EM-3, 1991 . . . .$9 – 12

Jaguar XJ12 Police, 4¾", King Size K-66, 1978 .$18 – 24

Jaguar XK150, 1960, DY-36, introduced in 1995
1. cream . . . .$18 – 24

Javelin AMX, 4¼", King Size K-54, 1975
1. burgundy . . . .$14 – 18
2. red . . . .$14 – 18
3. black . . . .$18 – 24

Javelin Drag Racing Set, 9¾", King Size K-57, 1975
1. K-54 Javelin with K-39 Milligan's Mill . . .$30 – 40
2. K-54 Javelin with K-38 Gus's Gulper . . .$30 – 40

JCB Excavator, 9⅞", King Size K-41, 1981; K-170, 1989,
Construction CS-9, 1991
1. K-41 . . . .$30 – 50
2. K-170 . . . .$20 – 30
3. CS-9 . . . .$20 – 30

Jennings Cattle Truck, 4¾", Major Pack M-7, 1960
1. gray plastic wheels . . . .$150 – 200
2. black plastic wheels . . . .$150 – 200

Kaman Seasprite Army Helicopter, 5⅞", Battle Kings
BK-118, 1978 . . . .$60 – 85

Karmann Ghia (see **Volkswagen Karmann Ghia**)

Kenworth, 7" tractor-trailer, Matchbox Collectibles
North American Brewmasters Collection
1. "Corona" . . . .$16 – 20

Kenworth Aerodyne, 7¾" tractor tanker trailer, Matchbox Collectibles Official Gas Tankers Collection
1. "Mobil" . . . .$20 – 30

Kenworth COE, 7" tractor-trailer, Matchbox Collectibles North American Brewmasters Collection
1. "Moosehead" . . . .$16 – 20

Kenworth Semi Tractor-Trailer, The Power of Harley,
1:58 scale, 12" . . . .$75 – 90

Kenworth Tanker, 12½", 1:58, Matchbox Collectibles
"The Spirit of Shell"; Exclusive Editions DYM-36838,
introduced in 1999
1. "Gulf," DYM-36838 . . . .$40 – 50
2. The Spirit of Shell . . . .$75 – 90

Kenworth W900, 5½", Matchbox Collectibles
Highway Commanders, 1:58 . . . .$35 – 50

King Tiger Tank, 4½", Battle Kings BK-104, 1974 . .$35 – 50

Kremer Porsche CK.5 Racer, 4¹/₁₆", Specials SP½,
1984; Super Kings K-1/K-2, 1989; also issued as Super
GT Sports, Turbo Specials, Muscle Cars, Alarm Cars,
Graffic Traffic, LA Wheels
1. black, "35 Porsche," LA Wheels . . . . .$14 – 18
2. maroon, "Michelin 15," Turbo Specials
TS3 . . . .$8 – 10
3. pearl silver, "19" and stripes, Specials SP2 . .$8 – 10
4. white, "22 Grand Prix," Specials SP1 . . .$8 – 10
5. white, "35 Porsche," Specials SP1 . . . .$8 – 10
6. white, "35 Porsche," Turbo Specials TS3 . .$8 – 10
7. white, "Lloyd's 1," British issue . . . .$25 – 40
8. white, green and yellow, "2," Specials
SP2 . . . .$8 – 10
9. white, no markings, Graffic Traffic . . . .$14 – 18

KW Dart Dump Truck, 5⅝", King Size
K-2-B, 1964 . . . .$75 – 100

Lagonda Drophead Coupe, 1938, Models of Yesteryear Y-11, introduced in 1973
1. beige with black chassis . . . .$18 – 24

2. copper with gold chassis . . . .**$18 – 24**
3. gold with purple chassis . . . .$900 – 1,000
4. gold with red chassis . . . .$400 – 500
5. gold with maroon chassis . . . .$50 – 60
6. plum with black interior . . . .$20 – 30
7. plum with maroon interior . . . .$35 – 40

Lamborghini Diablo, King Size K-173, 1992
    1. black . . . .$9 – 12
    2. yellow . . . .$9 – 12

Lamborghini Miura, 4", King Size K-24, 1969
    1. blue . . . .$15 – 20
    2. burgundy . . . .$15 – 20
    3. metallic bronze . . . .$15 – 20
    4. red . . . .$40 – 60

Lamp Maintenance Set, King Size K-93, 1982 .$16 – 20

Lancia Rallye, 4⁷⁄₁₆", Specials SP5/6, 1984; Super Kings K-5, 1989; also issued as Super GT Sports, Turbo Specials, Muscle Cars, Alarm Cars, Graffic Traffic, LA Wheels
    1. dark blue, "Pirelli 16," LA Wheels . . . . . .$8 – 10
    2. green, "Pirelli 116," Specials SP5 . . . .$8 – 10
    3. white, "102," Turbo Specials TS5 . . . .$8 – 10
    4. white, "Martini Racing 1," Specials SP6 . .$8 – 10
    5. white, no markings, Graffic Traffic . . . .$14 – 18
    6. yellow, "102," Specials SP5 . . . .$8 – 10

Land Rover Fire Engine, 1952, Matchbox Collectibles Fire Engine Collection YFE-02, introduced in 1994; YFE-25, introduced in 1999

    1. red, YFE-02 . . . .**$25 – 30**
    2. yellow, YFE-02 . . . .$90 – 110
    3. dark blue, "Royal Navy Rescue," YFE-25 . .$40 – 55

Land Rover Fire Truck (see Land Rover Fire Engine)

Land Rover Pilot Car, King Size K-144, 1987
    1. green, "Veterinary Surgeon," Great
       Britain issue . . . .$18 – 24
    2. orange, "Heathrow Airport," Great
       Britain issue . . . .$9 – 12
    3. orange, "Road Maintenance," U.S. issue . .$9 – 12
    4. yellow, "Frankfurt Flughafen,"
       Germany issue . . . .$9 – 12

Land Rover Series 1, 1949, The Dinky Collection DY-9, introduced in 1989

    1. green . . . .**$12 – 16**
    2. yellow, "AA Road Service" . . . .$18 – 24

Leyland 3-Ton Lorry, 1920, Models of Yesteryear Y-9, introduced in 1985

Leyland 4-Ton Van, 1914, Models of Yesteryear Y-7, introduced in 1957
    1. three lines of text, cream roof, black
       plastic wheels . . . .$1,250 – 1,500
    2. three lines of text, cream roof,
       metal wheels . . . .$80 – 100
    3. three lines of text, white roof,
       metal wheels . . . .$80 – 100
    4. two lines of text, cream roof,
       metal wheels . . . .$900 – 1,000

Leyland Car Recovery Vehicle, King Size
    K-140, 1987 . . . .$9 – 12

Leyland Car Transporter, King Size K-120, 1986 .$18 – 24

Leyland Cement Truck, King Size K-123, 1986;
Construction CS-3, 1991 . . . .$9 – 12

Leyland Cub Fire Engine
1. YFE-08, Matchbox Collectibles Fire Engine
    Collection, introduced in 1995 . . . . .$25 – 30
2. YSFE-02, Matchbox Collectibles Fire Engine
    Collection, introduced in 1996 . . . . .$50 – 60

Leyland Cub Hook and Ladder Truck, 1936, Models
of Yesteryear Y-9, introduced in 1989 . .$125 – 150

**Leyland Skip Truck, King Size K-151, 1988;
Construction CS-4, 1991** . . . .$9 – 12

Leyland Tipper, 4½", King Size K-4, 1970; K-37, 1979
1. dark red cab, metallic silver dumper, "LE Trans-
    port" labels, black plastic tires, K-4 . .$15 – 20
2. dark red cab, metallic silver dumper, "W.
    Wates" labels, black plastic tires, K-4 . .$40 – 55
3. orange-red cab, metallic lime green
    dumper, "W. Wates" labels, black plastic
    tires, K-4 . . . .$55 – 70
4. orange-red cab, metallic lime green
    dumper, "W. Wates" labels, Superfast
    wheels, K-4 . . . .$25 – 40
5. orange-red cab, metallic lime green dumper,
    no labels, Superfast wheels, K-4 . . . .$25 – 40

6. yellow with red dumper, "Laing," K-37 . . . .$14 – 18

7. orange-red cab, pea green dumper, "W.
    Wates" labels, black plastic tires, K-4 . .$40 – 55
8. pale blue cab, metallic silver dumper, miner
    and cave graphics, Superfast wheels,
    Mexico issue, K-4 . . . .$60 – 85
9. pale green cab and dumper, "W. Wates"
    labels, black plastic tires, K-4 . . . . .$500 – 750

Leyland Titan TD1 London Bus, 1929, Models of Yesteryear Y-5, introduced in 1989; Matchbox Collectibles European Transports YET-02, introduced in
1996
1. "MICA for collectors of Matchbox,"
    maroon . . . .$30 – 40
2. "Newcastle Brown Ale," maroon . . . . .$18 – 24
3. "Robin, The New Starch," lime green . .$18 – 24
4. "Swan Fountpens," blue, issued in frame with one
    assembled and one disassembled . .$80 – 100
5. "Van Houten's Cocoa," YET-02 . . . . . .$24 – 32

Leyland Truck with three interchangeable backs,
King Size K-150, 1988
1. blue cab . . . .$18 – 24
2. yellow cab . . . .$12 – 16

Lightning, 4¼", King Size K-35, 1972
1. red, "35 Team Matchbox" . . . .$15 – 20
2. red, "Flame Out," UK issue . . . .$180 – 240
3. white, "35 Team Matchbox" . . . .$15 – 20
4. white, "35 STP Champion" . . . .$15 – 20

Lincoln Zephyr, 1938, Models of Yesteryear Y-64,
introduced in 1992; Matchbox Collectibles Cars of
the Rich & Infamous DYM-35180, introduced in 1999
1. cream, Y-64 . . . .$40 – 55

2. light rose, DYM-35180 . . . .$30 – 40
3. purple, Y-64 . . . .$20 – 30

Log Transporter (see **Mercedes Benz Log Transporter**)

London Bus (see **Leyland Titan TD1 London Bus**)

London Bus, 1911 B Type, Models of Yesteryear Y-2,
introduced in 1956

1. eight over four windows . . . .$65 – 80
2. four over four side windows . . . .$250 – 300

London E Class Tram Car, 1907, Models of Yesteryear Y-3, introduced in 1956
    1. "Dewar's" . . . .$475 – 500

2. "News of the World" . . . .$60 – 80

London Horse Drawn Bus, 1899, Models of Yesteryear Y-12, introduced in 1959

1. beige driver and seats . . . .$65 – 75
2. light pink driver and seats . . . .$80 – 90

London Omnibus, Matchbox Collectibles "Historical Series" Collection YHS-02, introduced in 1993 . . . .$60 – 75

Londoner Bus (see **The Londoner**)

Lotus Super Seven, 1961, DYB-07, introduced in 1998
    1. red with black doors . . . .$24 – 32

Low Loader with Bulldozer (see **Ford Tractor with Dyson Low Loader and Case Tractor Bulldozer, Scammell Crusader Low Loader with Bulldozer**)

M3A1 Half Track APC, 3⅞", Battle Kings
    BK-108, 1974 . . . .$35 – 50

M48A2 Tank, 4⅝", Battle Kings BK-102, 1974 .$35 – 50

M551 Sheridan Tank, 4⅛", Battle Kings
    BK-109, 1975 . . . .$35 – 50

Mack 7" Tractor-trailer, Matchbox Collectibles North American Brewmasters Collection
    1. "Honey Brown Lager" . . . .$16 – 20

Mack AC Tanker, 1930, Models of Yesteryear Y-23, introduced in 1989; YFE-11, Matchbox Collectibles Fire Engine Collection, introduced in 1996
    1. "Conoco" . . . .$16 – 24
    2. "Texaco" . . . .$16 – 24
    3. Fire Tanker . . . .$20 – 30

Mack AC Truck, 1920, Models of Yesteryear Y-30, introduced in 1985; Y-33, introduced in 1990; Matchbox Collectibles "Great Beers of the World" Collection YGB-09, introduced in 1994; YGB-23, introduced in 1996; "Power of the Press" YPP-06, introduced in 1995; Charity series YCH-06, introduced in 1998; YPC-03, introduced in 1998

1. "Acorn Storage," light blue, Y-30 . . . . .$18 – 24
2. "Arctic Ice Cream," cream, Y-30 . . . . .$18 – 24
3. "Coca-Cola," "Stoneleigh Pharmacy Drink Coca-Cola," black, YPC-03 . . . .$30 – 40
4. "Goodyear," blue, Y-33 . . . .$18 – 24
5. "Kiwi Boot Polish," red, Y-30 . . . .$18 – 24
6. "Moosehead Beer," YGB-09 . . . .$18 – 24

7. "Pravda," YPP-06 . . . .**$20 – 30**
8. "Ronald McDonald House," white and red,
   YCH-06, Australia issue . . . .$30 – 40
9. "Tsingtau Beer," YGB-23 . . . .$18 – 24

Mack B, 1956, Matchbox Collectibles Big Rig Cabs DYM35214, introduced in 1999; Classic 1950s Automobilia DYM-35265, DYM-35266, DYM-35268, introduced in 1999
1. "Champion," DYM-35268 . . . .$30 – 40
2. "Pennzoil," DYM-35265 . . . .$30 – 40
3. "Texaco," DYM-35266 . . . .$30 – 40
4. yellow with black fenders, DYM-35214 . .$40 – 50

Mack B Tractor-Trailer, 1956; Matchbox Collectibles Tractor Trailers DYM-34557, issued 2000
1. "McDonald's" . . . .$80 – 100

Mack Canvasback Truck, 1920, Models of Yesteryear Y-30, introduced in 1985
1. "Consolidated Transport," yellow . . . .$18 – 24

Mack CH600, 5¾", Matchbox Collectibles Highway Commanders; Budweiser Rigs DYM-36672, introduced in 1998

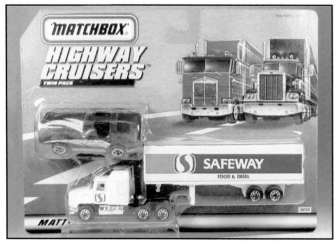

**1. "Safeway," Highway Cruisers Safeway
Exclusive** . . . .**$12 – 16**

2. "Bud Lite," DYM-36672 . . . .$48 – 54
3. Highway Commanders . . . .$35 – 50

Mack CH600, 7¾" tractor tanker trailer, Matchbox Collectibles Official Gas Tankers Collection
1. "Citgo" . . . .$20 – 30
2. "Shell" . . . .$20 – 30

Mack Fire Engine, 1911, 5⅞", YFE-01, Matchbox Collectibles Fire Engine Collection, introduced in 1994 . . . .$30 – 40

Mack Model AC (see **Mack AC Truck, Mack AC Tanker**)

Mack Petrol Tanker (see **Mack AC Tanker**)

Mack Pumper, 1911, Matchbox Collectibles Fire Engine Collection YFE-24, introduced in 1998 . . . .$35 – 50

Mack Pumper, 1935, Matchbox Collectibles Fire Engine Collection YFE-15, introduced in 1997 . . . .$35 – 50

Magirus Deutz Fire Engine, King Size K-110, 1985; K-132 with roof lights that steer front wheels, 1986 . . . .**$9 – 12**

Marauder, 4⅛", King Size K-45, 1973 . . . .$14 – 18

Maserati 250F, 1957, Models of Yesteryear Y-10, introduced in 1986 . . . .$18 – 24

Maserati Bora, 4", King Size K-56, 1975
1. metallic gray . . . .$14 – 18
2. metallic gold . . . .$70 – 90
3. red . . . .$18 – 24

Massey Ferguson Combine Harvester, 4⅝", Major Pack M-5, 1959
    1. orange plastic front wheels, black plastic rear wheels . . . .$100 – 125
    2. orange plastic front and rear wheels $100 – 125
    3. silver metal front wheels, black plastic rear wheels . . . .$100 – 125
    4. yellow plastic front wheels, black plastic rear wheels . . . .$700 – 900
    5. yellow plastic front and rear wheels .$100 – 125

Massey Ferguson Farm Set, tractor with accessories, Action Farming FM-8, 1991 . . . .$18 – 24

Massey Ferguson Tractor (see **Massey Ferguson Tractor and Hay Trailer, Massey Ferguson Tractor and Rotary Rake, Massey Ferguson Tractor and Trailer, Massey Ferguson Farm Set**)

Massey Ferguson Tractor and Hay Trailer, 8⅞", King Size K-35, 1979; Action Farming FM-6, 1991
    1. red, England cast . . . .$18 – 24
    2. red, Early Learning Centre, Macau cast . .$14 – 18
    3. red, FM-6, China cast . . . .$14 – 18

Massey Ferguson Tractor and Rotary Rake, King Size K-87, 1981; Action Farming FM-7, 1991
    1. red with orange frame, K-87 . . . .$18 – 24
    2. green with green frame, FM-7 . . . . . .$14 – 18

Massey Ferguson Tractor and Trailer, 8", King Size K-3, 1970 . . . .$35 – 60

Matchbox Racing Car Transporter (see **Racing Car Transporter, Matchbox**)

Matra Rancho, King Size K-90, 1982; Emergency EM-2, 1991
    1. red, "Fire Control Unit," EM-2 . . . .$9 – 12
    2. red, China cast, K-90 . . . .$9 – 12
    3. red, England cast, K-90 . . . .$14 – 18
    4. red, Macau cast, K-90 . . . .$12 – 15
    5. white, England cast, part of K-104 . . . . .$9 – 12
    6. yellow, England cast, K-90 . . . .$14 – 18

Matra Rancho Rescue Set, King Size K-104, 1983; K-109, 1984
    1. packaged as K-104, 1983 . . . .$20 – 30
    2. packaged as K-109, 1984 . . . .$30 – 40

Maxwell Roadster, 1911, Models of Yesteryear Y-14, introduced in 1965; Medallion Series YMS-06, introduced in 1996
    1. beige . . . .$18 – 24
    2. gold plated . . . .$50 – 60
    3. red with gold pinstripe trim, YMS-06 . . .$20 – 30

    4. silver plated . . . .$50 – 60
    5. turquoise with gold gas tank . . . .$40 – 60

6. turquoise with copper gas tank . . . . . .$20 – 30

McCormick International Tractor, 2¹³⁄₁₆", King Size K-4, 1960
    1. red with black plastic tires on green metal hubs . . . .$65 – 90
    2. red with black plastic tires on orange plastic hubs . . . .$65 – 90
    3. red with black plastic tires on red metal hubs . . . .$65 – 90

4. red with black plastic tires on red plastic hubs . . . .$65 – 90

Mercedes, 1908 Grand Prix, Models of Yesteryear Y-10, introduced in 1958

1. cream . . . .$70 – 85

2. white . . . . $125 – 150

Mercedes Benz 190E 2.3 16V, King Size K-115, 1985
    1. black . . . .$8 – 10
    2. metallic gray . . . .$8 – 10

3. metallic light blue . . . .**$8 – 10**

4. metallic light green . . . .**$8 – 10**
5. white, England cast . . . .$9 – 12
6. white, "Fuji," Macau cast . . . .$8 – 10
7. white, "Fuji," China cast . . . .$8 – 10

Mercedes Benz 190E Police, Emergency
    EM-15, 1993 . . . .$9 – 12

Mercedes Benz 190E Taxi, King Size K-166, 1989 .$8 – 10

Mercedes Benz 300SL "Gullwing," 1955, The Dinky
Collection DY-12, introduced in 1990; DY-924, introduced in 1992
    1. black, DY-12 . . . .$12 – 16
    2. pewter, DY-924 . . . .$40 – 50
    3. white, DY-12 . . . .$20 – 30

Mercedes Benz 300SL Convertible, 1962, The Dinky
Collection DY-33, introduced in 1995
    1. dark blue . . . .$18 – 24

Mercedes Benz 350SLC, 4⅛", King Size K-48, 1973
    1. metallic copper . . . .$14 – 18
    2. metallic gray with black roof (part of K-2
        Car Recovery Vehicle) . . . .$14 – 18

Mercedes Benz 36/220, 1928, Models of Yesteryear
Y-10, introduced in 1963
    1. cream . . . .$75 – 80
    2. gold plated . . . .$50 – 60
    3. silver plated . . . .$50 – 60

4. white . . . .**$120 – 140**

Mercedes Benz 500SL, King Size K-172, 1991; Ultra
Class, 1991
    1. metallic gray . . . .$8 – 10
    2. metallic red . . . .$8 – 10
    3. red, Ultra Class . . . .$14 – 18

Mercedes Benz 540K, 1937, Models of Yesteryear Y-20,
introduced in 1981

1. black with chrome spoked wheels . . . . . .**$20 – 30**
2. metallic gray with red disk wheels . . . .$30 – 40

3. metallic gray with red spoked wheels . . .$30 – 40
4. metallic gray with silver disk wheels . . .$25 – 30

5. metallic gray with silver spoked wheels . . . .$14 – 18
6. red with red spoked wheels . . . .$18 – 24
    with diorama . . . .$20 – 30
7. white with red spoked wheels . . . .$18 – 24

Mercedes Benz 770, Matchbox Models of Yesteryear Y-40, introduced in 1991; Matchbox Collectibles Y-53, introduced in 1998; Matchbox Collectibles Cars of the Rich & Infamous DYM-35185, introduced in 1999

1. black with white roof, DYM-35185 . . . .$30 – 40

2. red with black roof, Y-40 . . . .$35 – 45
3. dark gray, Y-40 . . . .$18 – 24
4. reddish brown, Y-53 . . . .$35 – 50

Mercedes Benz Ambulance (see **Mercedes Benz "Binz" Ambulance**)

Mercedes Benz "Binz" Ambulance, King Size K-6, 1967; K-26, 1971; K-63, 1977
    1. black plastic tires on silver hubs, K-6 . .$30 – 50
    2. Superfast wheels, K-26 or K-63 . . . .$14 – 18

Mercedes Benz Bus, 1950, The Dinky Collection
    DY-10, introduced in 1989 . . . .$60 – 80

Mercedes Benz Container Truck, King Size K-124, 1986
    1. white cab, "7-Up" . . . .$18 – 24
    2. metallic gray, "Taglich Frisch,"
       Germany issue . . . .$40 – 50

Mercedes Benz Crane Truck, King Size
    K-148, 1988 . . . .$16 – 20

Mercedes Benz Farm Unimog and Livestock Trailer, 8⅞", King Size K-32, 1978 . . . .$15 – 20

Mercedes Benz Garage Transporter, King Size
    K-135, 1986 . . . .$20 – 30

Mercedes Benz KS15 Fire Engine, YFE-07, Matchbox Collectibles Fire Engine Collection, introduced in 1995 . . . .$25 – 30

Mercedes Benz L5 Truck, 1932, Models of Yesteryear Y-6, introduced in 1988; Y-41, introduced in 1991; Matchbox Collectibles "Great Beers of the World" Collection YGB-06, introduced in 1993; YGB-17, introduced in 1995; YGB-21, introduced in 1996; Matchbox Collectibles "Power of the Press" YPP-03, introduced in 1996; Matchbox Collectibles Charity series YCH-08, introduced in 1998
    1. "DAB Pils-Das Bier Von Weltreut,"
       YGB-21 . . . .$18 – 24
    2. "Henniger-Brau," YGB-17 . . . .$18 – 24
    3. "Holsten Brauerei," YGB-06 . . . .$18 – 24
    4. "Howaldtswerks AG Kiel," Y-41 . . . .$18 – 24

5. "Morgenpost," YPP-03 . . . .$20 – 30

6. "Ronald McDonald House," yellow and red,
YCH-08, Australia issue . . . .$30 – 40
7. "Stuttgarter Hofbrau," Y-6 . . . .$18 – 24

Mercedes Benz Ladder Truck, YFE-05, Matchbox
Collectibles Fire Engine Collection, introduced
in 1995 . . . .$25 – 30

Mercedes Benz Log Transporter, 12⅝", King Size K-43, 1981
1. yellow with orange boom, brown logs, Eng-
land cast . . . .$20 – 30

Mercedes Benz Lorry (see **Mercedes Benz Truck**)

Mercedes Benz Pipe Transporter, 12⅝", Construction
CS-11, 1991
1. yellow with red boom, gray pipes,
China cast . . . .$16 – 20

Mercedes Benz Police Car, 4¼", King Size K-61, 1976
1. white with green hood and doors,
"Polizei," Germany issue . . . .$30 – 40
2. white with white hood and doors,
"Police" . . . .$14 – 18

Mercedes Benz Power Launch Transporter, King Size
K-129, 1986; Emergency EM-12, 1991
1. K-129 . . . .$18 – 24
2. EM-12 . . . .$14 – 18

Mercedes Benz SS Coupe, 1928, Models of Yesteryear Y-16, introduced in 1972
1. blue and gray with blue chassis,
black roof . . . .$20 – 30
2. blue and light blue with blue chassis,
black roof . . . .$20 – 30
3. blue and beige with blue chassis,
black roof . . . .$20 – 30
4. dark green with dark green chassis,
black roof . . . .$18 – 24
5. light green with emerald green chassis,
black roof . . . .$175 – 225
6. light green with light green chassis,
black roof . . . .$18 – 24
7. light green with light green chassis,
green roof . . . .$125 – 150

8. metallic gray with red chassis, black roof . . . .$60 – 75

9. white with white chassis, black roof . .$18 – 24

Mercedes Benz Truck, 1920, Matchbox Collectibles
Y-32, introduced in 1998
1. "O'Neill Family Products" . . . .$35 – 50

Mercedes Benz Truck, 1932 (see **Mercedes Benz L5
Truck, 1932**)

Mercedes Benz Type 770, 1931 (see **Mercedes Benz
770**)

Mercedes Benz Unimog and Compressor, 7¼", King
Size K-30, 1978
1. beige . . . .$16 – 20
2. gray . . . .$30 – 50

Mercedes Benz Unimog Snow Plow, King Size K-163,
1989
1. orange, China cast . . . .$10 – 13
2. orange, Macau cast . . . .$12 – 16

Mercedes Benz Unimog Tar Sprayer, Construction
CS- 5, 1991 . . . .$9 – 12

Mercer Raceabout, 1913, Models of Yesteryear Y-7,
introduced in 1961
1. gold plated with gold grille . . . .$225 – 250
2. lilac with gray tires . . . .$100 – 125

3. lilac with black tires . . . .**$40 – 60**
4. silver plated with silver grille . . . .$180 – 200
5. yellow with yellow grille . . . .$24 – 32
6. yellow with gold grille . . . .$24 – 32

Mercury Capri (see **Ford Capri Mk 2**)

Mercury Commuter and Dodge Dragster (see **Drag
Pack**)

Mercury Commuter and Lightning Racer (see **Race
Pack**)

Mercury Commuter and Thunderclap Racer (see
Race Pack)

Mercury Commuter Police Station Wagon, 4⅜", King Size K-23, 1969
    1. white with black plastic tires . . . .$50 – 70
    2. white with Superfast wheels . . . .$25 – 40

Mercury Commuter Station Wagon (see **Drag Pack, Race Pack**)

Mercury Cougar, 4⅛", King Size K-21, 1968
    1. metallic gold with red interior . . . . . .$60 – 85
    2. metallic gold with white interior . . . . .$80 – 110

Mercury Cougar Dragster, 4⅛", K-21, 1971
    1. burgundy, "Dinamite" . . . .$18 – 24
    2. pink, "Dinamite" . . . .$18 – 24
    3. purple, "Bender" . . . .$20 – 30
    4. purple, "Dinamite" . . . .$18 – 24

Merryweather Fire Engine, 6", King Size K-15, 1964

    1. red with black plastic tires on
       red plastic hubs . . . .**$70 – 90**
    2. red with Superfast wheels . . . .$40 – 60
    3. metallic red with Superfast wheels . . .$40 – 60

Merryweather Fire Engine, 1868, Models of Yester-year Y-46, introduced in 1991; Matchbox Collectibles Special Fire Engine Collection YSFE-05
    1. red, "Tehidy House," with firemen, Y-46 . .$50 – 60
    2. red, no markings, no firemen, YSFE-05 . .$60 – 80

Merryweather Fire Engine, 1904, Matchbox Collectibles Fire Engine Collection YFE-19, introduced in 1998 . . . .$30 – 40

Messerschmitt KR200, 1955, VEM-04, introduced in 1997

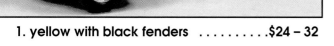

    1. yellow with black fenders . . . .**$24 – 32**

MGB, DYB-05, introduced in 1998
    1. pale yellow with black roof . . . .$24 – 32

MGB GT, 1965, The Dinky Collection DY-3, introduced in 1989
    1. blue with black roof . . . .$12 – 16
    2. orange . . . .$12 – 16

MGB GT V-8, 1973, The Dinky Collection DY-19, introduced in 1990
    1. red . . . .$18 – 24
    2. reddish brown . . . .$12 – 16

MG TD, 1945, Models of Yesteryear Y-8, introduced in 1978
    1. green with tan roof, red
       12-spoked wheels . . . .$30 – 40
    2. green with tan roof, silver
       12-spoked wheels . . . .$18 – 24
    3. green with tan roof, tan interior, silver
       24-spoked wheels . . . .$75 – 90
    4. green with tan roof, black interior, silver
       24-spoked wheels . . . .$60 – 75
    5. red with tan roof, red interior, silver
       24-spoked wheels . . . .$60 – 75
    6. red with tan roof, black interior, silver
       24-spoke wheels . . . .$14 – 18
    7. red with brown roof, black interior, silver
       24-spoke wheels . . . .$14 – 18
    8. blue with tan roof . . . .$14 – 18

    9. cream with tan roof . . . .**$14 – 18**

Military Ambulance (see **DAF Ambulance**)

Military Crane Truck, 6⅛", Battle Kings BK-113, 1977 . . . .$55 – 80

Military Tank (see **M48A2 Tank**, **Chieftain Tank**, **King Tiger Tank**)

Milligan's Mill, 4½", K-39, 1973
    1. dark green, flames label on roof, orange
       interior and rollbar, blue windows . . .$14 – 18

2. dark green, flames label on roof, orange
   interior and rollbar, clear windows ..$14 – 18
3. dark green, flames label on roof, yellow
   interior and rollbar, clear windows ..$14 – 18
4. dark green, stars and stripes label on roof, orange
   interior and rollbar, clear windows ..$16 – 20
5. light green, flames label on roof, orange
   interior and rollbar, clear windows ..$14 – 18

Mini Cooper S, 1964 (see **Austin Mini Cooper S, 1964**)

Missile Launcher, 4⅜", Battle Kings BK-111, 1975 ..$40 – 65

Mobile Crane, King Size K-114, 1985; Construction
CS-8, 1991 ....$18 – 24

Mobilgas Petrol Tanker, 3⅞", Major Pack M-8, 1960
1. gray plastic tires ....$175 – 225
2. black plastic tires ....$475 – 525

Mod Tractor and Trailer, 7¾", King Size K-3, 1974
1. blue-green, no labels ....$65 – 90
2. metallic blue, star inside circle label ..$65 – 90
3. metallic blue, stars and stripes labels ..$20 – 30

Morgan, 1955, DYB-03, introduced in 1998
1. black ....$24 – 32

Morris 10 CWT Van, 1929, Models of Yesteryear Y-19,
introduced in 1987; Y-47, introduced in 1991
1. "Antiques Road Show 1991," black
   with yellow roof ....$1,750 – 2,000
2. "Brasso," blue, China cast ....$30 – 40
3. "Brasso," blue, Macau cast ....$18 – 24
4. "Chocolat Lindt," black with yellow roof ..$18 – 24
5. "Michelin," blue ....$18 – 24
6. "Sainsbury," brown ....$18 – 24

**Morris Cowley Bullnose, 1926, Models of Yesteryear
Y-8, introduced in 1958** ....$60 – 80

Morris Light Van, 1929, Matchbox Collectibles "Great
Beers of the World" Collection YGB-04, introduced in
1993; YWG-03, introduced in 1997

1. "Cutty Sark Scots Whisky," yellow,
   YWG-03 ....$20 – 30
2. "Fuller's," green, YGB-04 ....$18 – 24

Morris Pantechicon, 1933, Models of Yesteryear Y-31,
introduced in 1990; Matchbox Collectibles "Great
Beers of the World" Collection YGB-18, introduced in
1995; "Power of the Press" YPP-02, introduced in
1995; Charity series YCH-09, introduced in 1998
1. "Cascade," YGB-18 ....$18 – 24
2. "Classic Toys For A Jolly Colorful Read" ..$60 – 80
3. "Kemp's Biscuits," Y-31 ....$16 – 20
4. "Ronald McDonald House," blue with dark
   blue roof and fenders, YCH-09,
   Australia issue ....$30 – 40

5. "The Times," YPP-02 ....$20 – 30
6. "Weetabix," Y-31 ....$16 – 20

Morris Van (see **Morris 10 CWT Van, Morris Light Van**)

Motor Coach (see **Camping Cruiser Motor Coach**)

Motorcycle Racing Set, King Size K-91, 1982
1. metallic gray Plymouth Gran Fury with two #33
   Honda CB750 motorcycles ....$40 – 60

Motorcycle Transporter, 4¾", King Size K-6, 1975 ..$12 – 16

Muir Hill Dumper, 3", King Size K-2, 1960
1. gray plastic tires on green metal hubs ..$75 – 90
2. black plastic tires on green metal hubs ..$75 – 90

Muir Hill Tractor and Trailer, 9½", King Size K-5-C, 1972
1. two-tone blue, Germany issue ....$50 – 75
2. yellow ....$25 – 40

Muir Tractor and Back Shovel, Action Farming
FM-2, 1991 ....$9 – 12

Muir Tractor and Back Shovel with Trailer, Action
Farming FM-5, 1991 ....$14 – 18

Mustang (see Ford Mustang II, Ford Cobra Mustang, Ford Mustang Boss 429)

Mustang Cobra (see Ford Cobra Mustang)

Nash Metropolitan, 1958, DYG-15, introduced in 1998; Matchbox Collectibles Oldies but Goodies II, issued 2004
    1. white and turquoise, DYG-15 . . . .$20 – 30
    2. white and turquoise, Oldies
       but Goodies II . . . .$9 – 12

Nissan 270ZX, 4", King Size K-42, 1973 . . . . . .$14 – 18

O & K Excavator, 4⅞", King Size K-1, 1970
    1. black plastic tires on red rims,
       amber windows . . . .$45 – 65
    2. Superfast wheels, amber windows . . .$20 – 25
    3. Superfast wheels, clear windows . . . .$20 – 25

Oldsmobile 442, 1970, Matchbox Collectibles Muscle Cars YMC-11, introduced in 1998
    1. white . . . .$30 – 40

Opel Coupe, 1909, Models of Yesteryear Y-4, introduced in 1966; Medallion Series YMS-03, introduced in 1996
    1. gold plated with red roof . . . .$50 – 60
    2. orange with black roof . . . .$20 – 30
    3. red with tan roof . . . .$20 – 30
    4. silver plated with red roof . . . .$50 – 60
    5. white with smooth tan roof,
       maroon seats . . . .$25 – 30

6. white with smooth tan roof, red seats . . . .**$20 – 30**
7. white with textured tan roof, red seats . .$40 – 60
8. yellow with black pinstripe trim, black
    roof, YMS – 03 . . . .$20 – 30

Packard Landaulet, 1912, Models of Yesteryear Y-11, introduced in 1964; Medallion Series YMS-04, introduced in 1996

1. beige and brown . . . .$20 – 30

2. red . . . .**$24 – 32**

3. pearl white, YMS-04 . . . .**$20 – 30**

Packard Victoria, 1930, Models of Yesteryear Y-15, introduced in 1969
    1. beige with white roof . . . .$40 – 60
    2. beige with tan roof . . . .$20 – 30
    3. beige with rust roof . . . .$30 – 35
    4. black and red with black roof . . . .$18 – 24

5. black and red with white roof . . . .**$14 – 18**
6. gold plated with maroon roof . . . . . .$50 – 60

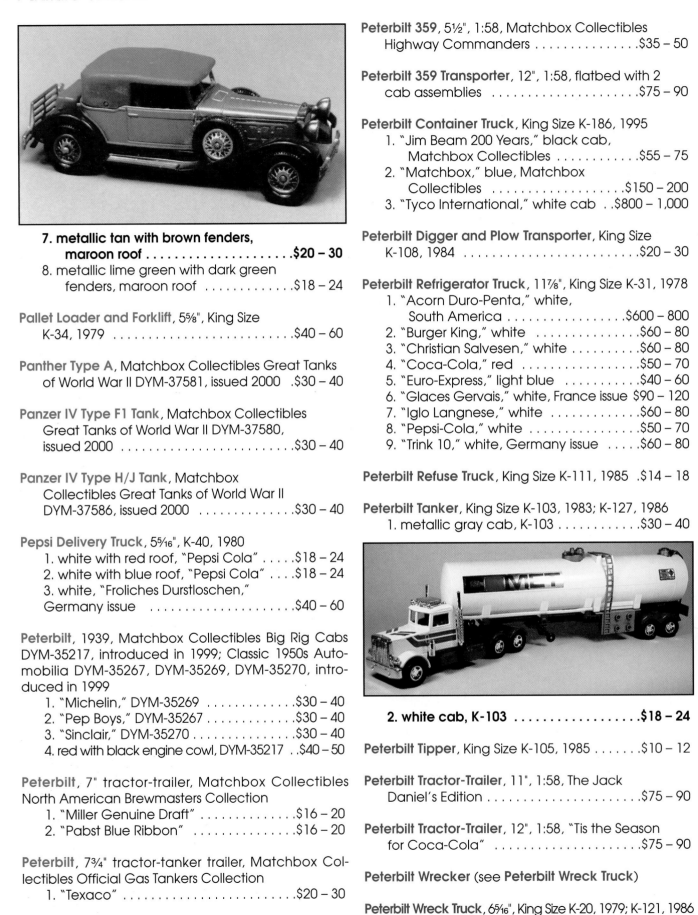

**7. metallic tan with brown fenders,
      maroon roof** . . . .**$20 – 30**
8. metallic lime green with dark green
    fenders, maroon roof . . . .$18 – 24

Pallet Loader and Forklift, 5⅝", King Size
    K-34, 1979 . . . .$40 – 60

Panther Type A, Matchbox Collectibles Great Tanks
    of World War II DYM-37581, issued 2000 .$30 – 40

Panzer IV Type F1 Tank, Matchbox Collectibles
    Great Tanks of World War II DYM-37580,
    issued 2000 . . . .$30 – 40

Panzer IV Type H/J Tank, Matchbox
    Collectibles Great Tanks of World War II
    DYM-37586, issued 2000 . . . .$30 – 40

Pepsi Delivery Truck, 5⁵⁄₁₆", K-40, 1980
    1. white with red roof, "Pepsi Cola" . . . . .$18 – 24
    2. white with blue roof, "Pepsi Cola" . . . .$18 – 24
    3. white, "Froliches Durstloschen,"
       Germany issue . . . .$40 – 60

Peterbilt, 1939, Matchbox Collectibles Big Rig Cabs
DYM-35217, introduced in 1999; Classic 1950s Automobilia DYM-35267, DYM-35269, DYM-35270, introduced in 1999
    1. "Michelin," DYM-35269 . . . .$30 – 40
    2. "Pep Boys," DYM-35267 . . . .$30 – 40
    3. "Sinclair," DYM-35270 . . . .$30 – 40
    4. red with black engine cowl, DYM-35217 ..$40 – 50

Peterbilt, 7" tractor-trailer, Matchbox Collectibles
North American Brewmasters Collection
    1. "Miller Genuine Draft" . . . .$16 – 20
    2. "Pabst Blue Ribbon" . . . .$16 – 20

Peterbilt, 7¾" tractor-tanker trailer, Matchbox Collectibles Official Gas Tankers Collection
    1. "Texaco" . . . .$20 – 30

Peterbilt 359, 5½", 1:58, Matchbox Collectibles
    Highway Commanders . . . .$35 – 50

Peterbilt 359 Transporter, 12", 1:58, flatbed with 2
    cab assemblies . . . .$75 – 90

Peterbilt Container Truck, King Size K-186, 1995
    1. "Jim Beam 200 Years," black cab,
       Matchbox Collectibles . . . .$55 – 75
    2. "Matchbox," blue, Matchbox
       Collectibles . . . .$150 – 200
    3. "Tyco International," white cab ..$800 – 1,000

Peterbilt Digger and Plow Transporter, King Size
    K-108, 1984 . . . .$20 – 30

Peterbilt Refrigerator Truck, 11⅞", King Size K-31, 1978
    1. "Acorn Duro-Penta," white,
       South America . . . .$600 – 800
    2. "Burger King," white . . . .$60 – 80
    3. "Christian Salvesen," white . . . .$60 – 80
    4. "Coca-Cola," red . . . .$50 – 70
    5. "Euro-Express," light blue . . . .$40 – 60
    6. "Glaces Gervais," white, France issue $90 – 120
    7. "Iglo Langnese," white . . . .$60 – 80
    8. "Pepsi-Cola," white . . . .$50 – 70
    9. "Trink 10," white, Germany issue . . . . .$60 – 80

Peterbilt Refuse Truck, King Size K-111, 1985 .$14 – 18

Peterbilt Tanker, King Size K-103, 1983; K-127, 1986
    1. metallic gray cab, K-103 . . . .$30 – 40

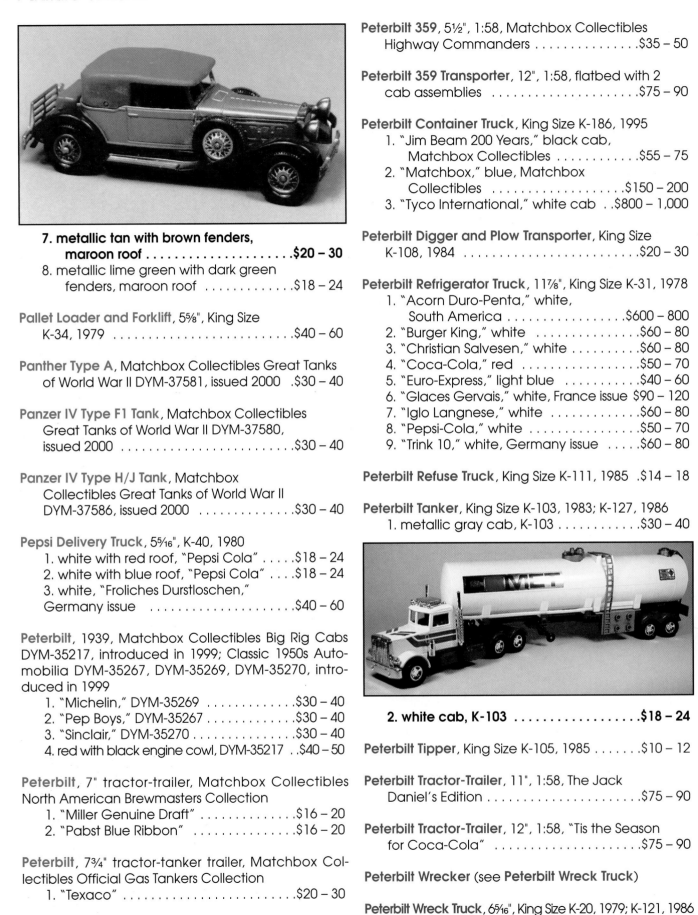

2. white cab, K-103 . . . .**$18 – 24**

Peterbilt Tipper, King Size K-105, 1985 . . . . . .$10 – 12

Peterbilt Tractor-Trailer, 11", 1:58, The Jack
    Daniel's Edition . . . .$75 – 90

Peterbilt Tractor-Trailer, 12", 1:58, "Tis the Season
    for Coca-Cola" . . . .$75 – 90

Peterbilt Wrecker (see Peterbilt Wreck Truck)

Peterbilt Wreck Truck, 6⁵⁄₁₆", King Size K-20, 1979; K-121, 1986

1. black and white, "Police," K-121 . . . . .$18 – 24
2. dark blue, K-121 . . . .$16 – 20
3. dark green, K-20 . . . .$18 – 24
4. lime green, K-20 . . . .$20 – 30
5. white, K-20 . . . .$60 – 80

Peterbilt Wreck Truck and Porsche 959, Emergency
EM-8, 1991 . . . .$14 – 18

Petrol Tanker (also see **Army Petrol Tanker**)

Petrol Tanker (see **Ford LTS Series Tractor and Articulated Tanker**)

Peugeot, 1907, Models of Yesteryear Y-5, introduced
in 1969
    1. bronze with black roof . . . .$125 – 150

2. bronze with bronze roof . . . .$20 – 30
3. metallic orange with metallic
        orange roof . . . .$20 – 30
4. metallic orange with black roof . . .$125 – 150

5. yellow with amber windows, black roof . . . .$20 – 30
6. yellow with clear windows, black roof . .$60 – 75

Peugeot 305, 4½", King Size K-84, 1981
    1. blue . . . .$14 – 18
    2. metallic blue . . . .$12 – 16
    3. white . . . .$12 – 16

Pickford 200-Ton Transporter, 11", Major
    Pack M-6, 1960 . . . .$175 – 225

Pipe Truck (also see **Log Transporter**)

Pipe Truck, 8", King Size K-10, 1967
    1. lavender with labels, gray pipes,
        Superfast wheels . . . .$25 – 40
    2. lavender with labels, yellow pipes,
        Superfast wheels . . . .$25 – 40
    3. metallic purple with labels, yellow pipes,
        Superfast wheels . . . .$25 – 40
    4. metallic purple with labels, orange pipes,
        Superfast wheels . . . .$25 – 40
    5. yellow with decals, gray pipes, black plastic
        tires on red hubs . . . .$60 – 80
    6. yellow with labels, gray pipes, black plastic
        tires on red hubs . . . .$60 – 80

Plymouth 'Cuda 440 6-Pack, Matchbox Collectibles
Muscle Cars YMC-02, introduced in 1997
    1. yellow . . . .$30 – 40

Plymouth Barracuda, 1971, Matchbox Collectibles
Budweiser Sports Cars DYM-37599, introduced in 1999
    1. Fly Fishing . . . .$30 – 40

Plymouth Gran Fury (also see **Motorcycle Racing Set**)

Plymouth Gran Fury Fire Chief Car, 5⅜", King Size
K-78, 1990
    1. maroon . . . .$9 – 12
    2. orange . . . .$9 – 12

3. red, "IAAFC," White Rose
   Collectibles promotional . . . .$14 – 18
4. white . . . .$9 – 12

Plymouth Gran Fury Police Car, 5⅜", King Size K-78, 1979; Emergency EM-1, 1991

1. **black and white, "City Police"** . . . .**$9 – 12**
2. black, blue interior, "Police" . . . .$24 – 36
3. black, white interior, "Police" . . . .$18 – 24
4. blue . . . .$14 – 18
5. blue and white, "Police" . . . .$14 – 18
6. blue and white, "Polizei" . . . .$14 – 18
7. white . . . .$9 – 12
8. yellow, EM-1 . . . .$8 – 10

Plymouth Gran Fury Taxi, 4⅜", King Size K-79, 1979
1. yellow . . . .$14 – 18

Plymouth GTX, 1970, Matchbox Collectibles Muscle Cars YMC-07, introduced in 1998
1. bright green with white stripes . . . . . .$30 – 40

Plymouth Road Runner Hemi, 1970, Matchbox Collectibles Muscle Cars YMC-04, introduced in 1997
1. metallic lime green . . . .$30 – 40

Plymouth Trail Duster Rescue Vehicle, 4½", King Size K-65, 1978
1. red, "Emergency Rescue" . . . .$14 – 18
2. green, "Bergrettungswacht,"
   Germany issue . . . .$40 – 60

Pontiac GTO, 1967, Matchbox Collectibles Muscle Cars YMC-03, introduced in 1997

1. **metallic light blue with dark blue roof** . . . .**$30 – 40**

Porsche 356A Coupe, 1958, The Dinky Collection DY-25, introduced in 1991
1. metallic gray . . . .$12 – 16

Porsche 911 Carrera, King Size K-168, 1989; Ultra Class, 1991
1. red . . . .$8 – 10
2. metallic white, Ultra Class . . . .$14 – 18

Porsche 944, King Size K-98, 1983 . . . .**$40 – 60**

Porsche Racing Car Transporter (see **Racing Car Transporter, Porsche**)

Porsche Turbo 944, King Size K-156, 1988
1. red, "Pioneer," "Elf," "18" . . . .$8 – 10

Porsche Turbo 944 Rally, King Size K-157, 1988
1. light orange, "Turbo Porsche 944" . . . . .$8 – 10

Porsche 959, 4⅜", Specials SP13/14, 1986; King Size K-11, 1989; Turbo Specials TS8; LA Wheels
1. black, "Michelin 44," unchromed rims,
   LA Wheels . . . .$8 – 10
2. black, "Turbo," chromed rims,
   Alarm Cars . . . .$16 – 20
3. dark blue, "Turbo," chromed rims,
   Alarm Cars . . . .$16 – 20
4. metallic silver, "3," stripes, unchromed rims,
   gray interior, King Size K-12 . . . .$14 – 18
5. metallic silver, "3," stripes, unchromed rims, tan
   interior, Turbo Specials TS8 . . . .$14 – 18
6. red, "Michelin 44," chromed rims, SP13 . .$8 – 10
7. red, cartoon design, white rims, Live 'N Learn/
   Matchbox Preschool . . . .$8 – 10
8. white, "53," stripes, chromed rims, SP14 .$8 – 10
9. white, "959," red, green and black lines $8 – 10
10. white, "Porsche 959," chromed rims,
    King Size K-11 . . . .$14 – 18
11. white, no markings, unchromed rims,
    Graffic Traffic . . . .$14 – 18
12. yellow, "53," stripes, unchromed rims,
    LA Wheels . . . .$8 – 10

Porsche 959 Racer, 4⅜", King Size K-12, 1989 (see Porsche 959)

Porsche Polizei, 4⅞", King Size K-71, 1979
1. white and green with two #33 Honda CB750 motorcycles, Germany issue . . . .$60 – 80

Porsche Turbo, 4⅝", King Size K-70, 1979

1. black . . . .$9 – 12
2. green . . . .$14 – 18
3. lime green . . . .$14 – 18
4. metallic red . . . .$9 – 12
5. red, Hong Kong issue . . . .$16 – 20

Power Boat and Trailer (see Seaburst Power Boat and Trailer)

Power Boat and Transporter, 10⅛", King Size K-27, 1978
1. orange, "Benihana" . . . .$18 – 24
2. orange, "Matchbox" . . . .$18 – 24
3. red, "Benihana" . . . .$18 – 24
4. red, "Miss Embassy" . . . .$18 – 24
5. red, "Matchbox" . . . .$18 – 24
6. white, "Benihana" . . . .$18 – 24
7. white, "Miss Embassy" . . . .$18 – 24
8. white, "Miss Solo" . . . .$18 – 24

Power Boat Transporter (see Mercedes Benz Power Launch Transporter, Power Boat and Transporter, Power Launch Transporter)

Power Launch Transporter, King Size K–107, 1984 . .$18 – 24

Preston London Tram, 1920, Models of Yesteryear Y–15, introduced in 1987; Matchbox Collectibles European Transports YET-01, introduced in 1996
1. "Golden Shred," orange, Y-15 . . . .$18 – 24
2. "Swan Soap," blue, Y-15 . . . .$18 – 24
3. "Swan Vestas," red, Y-15 . . . .$18 – 24
   disassembled in framed display . . .$80 – 100
4. "Yorkshire Relish," blue, YET-01 . . . . . .$24 – 32
5. "Zebra Grate," brown, Y-15 . . . .$18 – 24

Prime Mover with Caterpillar Crawler, 12½", King Size K-8, 1962 . . . .$200 – 250

Prince Henry Vauxhall, 1914, Models of Yesteryear Y-2, introduced in 1970; Medallion Series YMS-07, introduced in 1996
1. blue with red seats . . . .$900 – 1,200

2. metallic blue with white seats . . . . . .$20 – 30
3. gold plated . . . .$50 – 60

4. green with gold pinstripe trim, YMS-07 . . . . .$20 – 30

5. metallic red with white seats . . . .$20 – 30
6. silver plated . . . .$50 – 60

Queen Elizabeth II's Gold State Coach (see Her Majesty Queen Elizabeth II's Gold State Coach)

Race Pack, 11", King Size K-46, 1973
1. Mercury Commuter and K-34 Thunderclap Racer . . . .$30 – 50
2. Mercury Commuter and K-35 Lightning Racer . . . .$30 – 50

Race Car Transporter (also see **Racing Car Transporter**)

Race Car Transporter, 5⅛", Major Pack M-6, 1965, King Size K-5, 1967

1. **green with black plastic tires on red rims, Major Pack M-6** . . . .**$50 – 75**
2. green with black plastic tires on red rims, King Size K-5 . . . .$45 – 60

Race Car Transporter, 6⅛", King Size K-7, 1973
   1. white, "Martini Racing," with #56 Hi-Tailer Team Matchbox Racer in red . . . .$45 – 60
   2. white, "Martini Racing," with #56 Hi-Tailer Team Matchbox Racer in white . . . .$35 – 50
   3. yellow, "Team Matchbox," with #34 Formula 1 Racing Car in pink . . . .$30 – 45
   4. yellow, "Team Matchbox," with #24 Team Matchbox Formula 1 Racer in green . .$65 – 90
   5. yellow, "Team Matchbox," with #24 Team Matchbox Formula 1 Racer in red . .$25 – 40
   6. yellow, "Team Matchbox," with #34 Formula 1 Racing Car in yellow . . . .$30 – 45

Race Rally Support Set, King Size K-102, 1983 .$18 – 24

Racing Car Transporter, Porsche, King Size K-159, 1988 . . . .$20 – 30

Racing Car Transporter, Matchbox, King Size K-160, 1989 . . . .$20 – 30

Racing Porsche, King Size K-101, 1983
   1. metallic beige . . . .$20 – 30
   2. red . . . .$9 – 12
   3. white . . . .$9 – 12

Raider Commander, 6⁵⁄₁₆", Adventure 2000 K-2001, 1977 . . . .$40 – 65

Rancho (see **Matra Rancho**)

Range Rover, King Size K-164, 1989, Action Farming FM-1, 1991
   1. beige, Great Britain issue . . . .$12 – 16
   2. dark blue . . . .$8 – 10
   3. dark green with sheep, shepherd, and dog, FM-1 . . . .$8 – 10
   4. white . . . .$8 – 10

Range Rover and Trailer (see **Forestry Range Rover and Trailer**)

Range Rover Fire Engine (see **Fire Control Range Rover**)

Range Rover Police, King Size K-165, 1989; Emergency EM-6, 1991 . . . .$9 – 12

Range Rover Police Set, King Size K-97, 1983 .$14 – 18

Range Rover Polizei Set, King Size K-99, 1979 .$90 – 120

Ready-Mix Concrete Truck (see **Foden Ready-Mix Concrete Truck**)

Recovery Vehicle, 5⅛", Battle Kings BK-110, 1975 . . . .$40 – 65

Refrigerator Truck (see **Peterbilt Refrigerator Truck**)

Refuse Truck (see **SD Refuse Truck**)

Renault AG (see **Renault Type AG**)

Renault 2-Seater, 1911, Models of Yesteryear Y–2, introduced in 1963

1. **green** . . . .**$24 – 32**
2. silver plated . . . .$50 – 60

Renault 4L, 1962, VEM-07, introduced in 1997
   1. blue-gray . . . .$24 – 32

Renault Bus, 1910, Models of Yesteryear Y-44, introduced in 1991
    1. orange-yellow with red roof,
       "Wesserling-Bassang" . . . .$80 – 100
    2. orange yellow with black roof,
       "Wesserling-Bassang" . . . .$18 – 24

Renault Type AG, 1910, Models of Yesteryear Y-25, introduced in 1983; Matchbox Collectibles "Great Beers of the World" Collection YGB-07, introduced in 1994; Matchbox Collectibles "Power of the Press" YPP-01, introduced in 1995; Matchbox Collectibles "European Transports" YET-06, introduced in 1996
    1. "British Red Cross Society-St. John
       Ambulance Association," olive . . . . .$20 – 30
    2. "Delhaize," green, Y-25 . . . .$18 – 24
    3. "Duckham's Oils," metallic gray, Y-25 . .$18 – 24
    4. "Eagle Pencils," light blue, Y-25 . . . . . .$18 – 24
    5. "James Neale & Sons," yellow, Y-25 . .$18 – 24
    6. "Kronenburg," YGB-07 . . . .$18 – 24

    7. "Le Figaro," YPP-01 . . . .$20 – 30
    8. "Perrier," green with gold spoked
       wheels, Y-25 . . . .$18 – 24
    9. "Perrier," green with red spoked
       wheels, Y-25 . . . .$30 – 40

    10. "St. Symphorien Coise Paris," pale
       green, YET-06 . . . .$24 – 32
    11. "Suchard Chocolat," lavender, Y-25 . .$18 – 24

    12. "Tunnock," red, Y-25 . . . .$18 – 24

REO Pickup, 1939, YTC-04, introduced in 1999
    1. cream . . . .$30 – 40

Riley MPH, 1934, Models of Yesteryear Y-3, introduced in 1974
    1. blue with 12-spoke silver wheels . . . . .$18 – 24
    2. metallic dark red with 24-spoke
       silver wheels . . . .$20 – 30
    3. metallic light red with 24-spoke
       silver wheels . . . .$20 – 30
    4. metallic light red with 12-spoke
       red wheels . . . .$30 – 40
    5. metallic purple with 24-spoke
       silver wheels . . . .$30 – 40
    6. metallic purple – red with 24 – spoke
       silver wheels . . . .$20 – 30
    7. metallic red with 12 – spoke silver wheels . .$50 – 60

RJ Racing Ferrari 512 BB (see **Ferrari 512 BB**)

Road Construction Set – Ford Truck, Compressor Trailer and Unimog, King Size K-118, 1985 .$40 – 50

Road Construction Set – DAF Truck, Compressor Trailer and Unimog, King Size K-137, 1986 .$40 – 50

Road Ripper (see **Caterpillar Traxcavator Road Ripper**)

Road Runner Hemi (see **Plymouth Road Runner Hemi**)

Rocket Launcher (see **Self Propelled Rocket Launcher**)

Rocket Striker, 4⅜", Adventure 2000 K-2004, 1977 . . . .$40 – 65

Rolls Royce, 1912, Models of Yesteryear Y-7, introduced in 1968
    1. gold plated . . . .$50 – 60
    2. metallic gold with red seats and grille . .$25 – 30
    3. metallic gold with black seats and grille . .$18 – 24
    4. metallic silver with ribbed gray roof . .$180 – 200
    5. metallic silver with ribbed red roof . . .$30 – 40
    6. metallic silver with smooth gray roof . .$24 – 32
    7. metallic silver with smooth red roof . . .$30 – 40
    8. silver plated . . . .$50 – 60
    9. yellow . . . .$14 – 18

Rolls Royce Armored Car, 1920, Models of Yesteryear Y-38, introduced in 1990 . . . .$25 – 30

Rolls Royce Fire Engine, 1920, Models of Yesteryear Y-6, introduced in 1977
    1. red with 12-spoke gold wheels,
       black seat . . . .$14 – 18

2. red with 12-spoke gold wheels,
   red seat . . . .$140 – 160

**3. red with 12-spoke silver wheels,
   black seat** . . . .**$20 – 30**
4. red with 24-spoke gold wheels,
   black seat . . . .$20 – 30

Rolls Royce Phantom I, 1926, Models of Yesteryear
Y-36, introduced in 1990 . . . .$18 – 24

Rolls Royce Silver Ghost, 1906, Models of Yesteryear
Y-10, introduced in 1969
   1. gold plated . . . .$50 – 60
   2. lime green . . . .$20 – 30
   3. silver plated . . . .$50 – 60
   4. silver with red wheels, maroon seats . .$20 – 30
   5. silver with red wheels, yellow seats . . .$25 – 30

6. white with silver wheels . . . .**$18 – 24**
7. white with red wheels . . . .$25 – 30

Rolls Royce Silver Ghost, 1907, Models of Yesteryear
Y-15, introduced in 1960
   1. gold plated with black tires . . . .$50 – 65

2. metallic pale green with black tires . . . .**$20 – 30**

3. metallic pale green with
   gray tires . . . .$50 – 65
4. silver plated with black tires . . . .$50 – 65

Rolls Royce Silver Spirit, King Size K-161, 1989
   1. metallic gray . . . .$8 – 10
   2. metallic red . . . .$12 – 15

Royal Mail Horse Drawn Coach, 1820, Models of
Yesteryear Y-39, introduced in 1990 . . . .$50 – 60

Ruston Bucyrus Power Shovel, 3⅞", Major Pack M-4,
1959
   1. gray or green treads, yellow or
      red decals . . . .$150 – 200

S. P. Howitzer (see **Self Propelled 155mm Howitzer**)

Sand Cat, 3⅜", King Size K-37, 1973
   1. orange . . . .$14 – 18
   2. red (from Car Recovery Vehicle,
      King Size K-2) . . . .$14 – 18
   3. gold plated, mounted on ashtray,
      Gift Ware . . . .$60 – 80

Santa Fe Locomotive (see **American General Locomotive**)

**Scammell 100-Ton Truck-Trailer with GER Class E 2-4-
0 Steam Locomotive**, 1929, Models of Yesteryear
YS-16, introduced in 1989 . . . .$80 – 100

Scammell Aircraft Transporter, King Size
K-106, 1984 . . . .$18 – 24

Scammell Articulated Container Truck, 9⅞", King Size
K-17, 1974
   1. blue cab, "Gentransco" . . . .$20 – 30
   2. blue cab, "Pppick-up a Penguin,"
      UK issue . . . .$20 – 30
   3. metallic red cab, "Gentransco" . . . . .$20 – 30
   4. metallic red, "Ginny Vogue Dolls,"
      U. S. issue . . . .$300 – 450
   5. white cab, "7-Up" . . . .$20 – 30
   6. yellow cab, "DBP,"
      Germany issue . . . .$40 – 60
   7. yellow cab, "Deutsche Bundespost,"
      Germany issue . . . .$40 – 60
   8. yellow cab, "Gentransco" . . . .$20 – 30

Scammell Container Truck, 5½", King Size K-14, 1971;
K – 24, 1977
   1. "LEP," K-14 . . . .$18 – 24
   3. "Gentransco," K-24 . . . .$16 – 20
   4. "Michelin," K-24 . . . .$16 – 20
   5. "Bauknecht Komplettkuchen,"
      Germany issue, K-24 . . . .$30 – 50

2. "Crowe," K-24 . . . .$14 – 18

1. "Kaffe DG Rich," dark blue, YET-04 . . .$24 – 32
2. dark green, Y-35 . . . .$24 – 32
3. red, Y-35 . . . .$24 – 32
4. white with porcelain Christmas tree on
    roof, YSC-01 . . . .$120 – 160
5. yellow, Y-16 . . . .$24 – 32

SD Refuse Truck, 4⅝", King Size K-7, 1967

**1. red cab, metallic gray container, "Cleansing
Service," black plastic tires** . . . . **$40 – 55**
2. red cab, metallic gray container, "Cleansing
    Service," Superfast wheels . . . .$20 – 30
3. dark blue, orange container, yellow,
    black and white labels, Superfast wheels,
    Mexico issue . . . .$60 – 85

Seaburst Power Boat and Trailer, 6", King Size
    K-25, 1971 . . . .$14 – 18

Seagrave AC53 Fire Engine, 1907, 4½", Matchbox
Collectibles Fire Engine Collection YFE-21, introduced in 1998
    1. white, "V.F.D." . . . .$35 – 50

Seasprite Army Helicopter (see **Kaman Seasprite
Army Helicopter**)

Security Truck, 12⅞", King Size K-19, 1979

Scammell Crane Truck, 6", King Size K-12, 1970
    1. orange with Superfast wheels $20-30
    2. silver-gray with Superfast wheels,
        Mexico issue . . . .$60 – 80
    3. yellow with black plastic tires on
        red plastic rims . . . .$45 – 60

Scammell Crusader Low Loader with Bulldozer, 11",
King Size K-23, 1974
    1. dark blue cab, "Hoch & Tief,"
        Germany issue . . . .$50 – 70
    2. metallic blue cab . . . .$20 – 30
    3. orange cab . . . .$20 – 30
    4. red cab . . . .$20 – 30
    5. yellow cab . . . .$20 – 30

Scammell Heavy Wreck Truck, 4¾", King Size K-2,
1969
    1. gold with amber windows . . . .$25 – 40
    2. white with amber windows . . . .$25 – 40
    3. white with green windows . . . .$90 – 120

Scammell Tipper Truck, 4¾", King Size K-19, 1967
    1. red cab, black plastic tires . . . .$50 – 70
    2. metallic red, Superfast wheels . . . .$30 – 50

Scania Digger Transporter, King Size K-130, 1986;
Construction CS-10, 1991
    1. K-130 . . . .$20 – 30
    2. CS-10 . . . .$14 – 18

Scania Transporter with Traxcavator Bulldozer,
    King Size K-117, 1985 . . . .$24 – 32

Scania Vabis Bus / Postbus, 1922, Models of Yester-
year Y-16, introduced in 1988; Matchbox Collectibles
Y-35, introduced in 1997; Matchbox Collectibles
European Transports YET-04, introduced in 1996;
Matchbox Collectibles Santa Claus Collection YSC-
01, introduced in 1995

1. white with yellow roof, "Group 4"
   labels . . . . $16 – 20
2. white with orange roof, "Group 4"
   labels . . . . $16 – 20
3. white with orange roof, "Fort Knox"
   labels . . . . $16 – 20

Sedan and Europa Caravan (see **Jaguar and Europa Caravan, Volvo and Europa Caravan**)

Self Propelled 155mm Howitzer, 4¼", Battle Kings BK-107, 1974 . . . . $35 – 50

Self Propelled Rocket Launcher, 4⅛", Battle Kings BK-117, 1977 . . . . $50 – 75

Sentinel Steam Wagon, Models of Yesteryear Y-4, introduced in 1956
1. black plastic wheels . . . . $200 – 250
2. unpainted metal wheels . . . . $50 – 60

Shand-Mason Horse Drawn Fire Engine with driver and two firemen, Models of Yesteryear Y-4, introduced in 1960
1. black horses, "London" . . . . $140 – 165
2. gray horses, "Kent" . . . . $275 – 300
3. white horses, "Kent" . . . . $150 – 175
4. white horses, "London" . . . . $140 – 165

Sheridan Tank (see **M551 Sheridan Tank**)

Sherman Tank, 3⅝", Battle Kings BK-101, 1974 .$35 – 50

Sherman M4A3 105mm Tank, Matchbox Collectibles Great Tanks of World War II DYM-37579, DYM-37585, issued 2000 . . . . $30 – 40

Shovel Nose, 4", King Size K-32, 1972
1. yellow with black interior,
   clear windows . . . . $14 – 18
2. yellow with black interior,
   amber windows . . . . $14 – 18
3. yellow with yellow interior,
   clear windows . . . . $20 – 30

Shovel Tractor with ducks, chicken, and rooster, Action Farming FM-3, 1991 . . . . $9 – 12

Showman's Engine, Matchbox Collectibles Steam-Powered Vehicles Collection . . . . $24 – 32

Shuttle Launcher, 4⅜", Adventure 2000 K-2006, 1982 . . . . $90 – 120

Simplex, 1912, Models of Yesteryear Y-9, introduced in 1968; Medallion Series YMS-08, introduced in 1996

1. **lime green with smooth tan roof** . . . . **$30 – 40**
2. dark green with smooth tan roof . . . . $30 – 40
3. dark green with textured tan roof . . . . $40 – 60

4. **dark red with gold pinstripe**
   trim, YMS-08 . . . . **$20 – 30**
5. metallic gold with textured black roof . . $50 – 60
6. pale gold with black roof . . . . $50 – 60
7. orange-red with black roof . . . . $18 – 24

8. **dark red with black roof** . . . . **$18 – 24**
9. dark red with yellow roof . . . . $18 – 24
10. yellow with black roof . . . . $14 – 18
    with diorama . . . . $18 – 24
11. yellow with yellow roof . . . . $20 – 30
    with diorama . . . . $30 – 35

Skip Truck (see **Leyland Skip Truck**)

Snorkel Fire Engine (see **ERF Simon Snorkel Fire Engine**)

Spyker, 1904, Models of Yesteryear Y-16, introduced in 1961
    1. light green with black tires . . . . .$1,600 – 2,000
    2. maroon with black tires . . . .$1,000 – 1,200
    3. yellow with gray tires . . . .$100 – 110
    4. yellow with black tires . . . .$24 – 32
    5. silver plated . . . .$50 – 60

SRN6 Hovercraft, 5", King Size K-22, 1974
    1. blue deck, white hull,
       "SRN6," "Seaspeed" . . . .$14 – 18
    2. white deck, black hull, "Calais-
       Ramsgate," "Hoverlloyd" . . . .$14 – 18
    3. white deck, black hull, "SRN6,"
       "Seaspeed" . . . .$14 – 18
    4. white deck, white hull, "SRN6,"
       "Seaspeed" . . . .$60 – 80

Stephenson's Rocket Steam Tractor and Wagon,
    YAS-01, Matchbox Collectibles Steam-Powered
    Vehicles Collection . . . .$24 – 32

Street Rod, 4", King Size K-50, 1973
    1. green . . . .$14 – 18
    2. orange with gold plated fenders, mounted on
       pen stand, Gift Ware . . . .$60 – 80

Studebaker Golden Hawk, 1958, The Dinky Collection DY-26, introduced in 1991; DYG-03, introduced in 1996; Matchbox Collectibles Oldies but Goodies I, issued 2004
    1. blue-green, DYG-03 . . . .$18 – 24
    2. blue, Oldies but Goodies I . . . .$9 – 12

3. metallic gold, DY-26 . . . .$18 – 24

Studebaker Pickup, 1938, YTC-05, introduced in 1999

1. yellow . . . .$30 – 40

Stutz, 1914, Models of Yesteryear Y-8, introduced in 1969
    1. blue with black roof . . . .$12 – 18

2. **metallic red with copper gas tank** . . .$20 – 30
    3. metallic red with gold gas tank . . . . .$60 – 75

Stutz Bearcat, 1931, Models of Yesteryear Y-14, introduced in 1974; Matchbox Collectibles Cars of the Rich & Infamous DYM-35179, introduced in 1999
    1. blue with chrome wheels, Y-14 . . . . . .$20 – 30
    2. cream and red with red wheels, Y-14 . .$30 – 40
    3. cream with silver wheels, Y-14 . . . . . .$18 – 24

4. metallic lime with silver wheels, Y-14 ....$18 – 24
5. yellow and black, DYM-35179 ......$30 – 40

Sunbeam Motorcycle and Milford Sidecar, Models of Yesteryear Y-8, introduced in 1962
    1. black sidecar seat ....$1,250 – 1,500
    2. bright green sidecar seat ....$400 – 500

3. dark green sidecar seat ....$40 – 60

Surtees F1 Racer, 4¼", King Size K-44, 1977; K-73, 1980
    1. white, "Chesterfield 18," K-44 on base ..$14 – 18
    2. white, "Chesterfield 18," K-73 on base ..$35 – 45
    3. light tan, K-73 on base ....$18 – 24

Suzuki Motorcycle and Rider, 4⁵⁄₁₆", King Size K-81, 1981
    1. white ....$14 – 18
    2. dark blue ....$14 – 18

Suzuki Santana / Samurai, King Size K-179, 1992, Emergency EM-14, 1993 ....$9 – 12

Suzuki Santana / Samurai Police, Emergency EM-14, 1991 ....$9 – 12

T-34/76 Tank, Matchbox Collectibles Great Tanks of World War II DYM-37583, issued 2000 ....$30 – 40

Talbot Van, 1927, Models of Yesteryear Y-5, introduced in 1978; Matchbox Collectibles "Great Beers of the World" Collection YGB-10, introduced in 1994
    1. "1st Dutch Swapmeet," blue and gray
      with black roof ....$275 – 325

2. "2nd AIM Convention," green with
    black roof ....$150 – 175
3. "AIM 25th Anniversary 1970-1995," black
    with yellow roof ....$50 – 60
4. "Bees Art," yellow with black roof ..$275 – 325
5. "Chivers," cream with green roof,
    red spoked wheels ....$14 – 18
6. "Chocolat Menier," blue with black roof,
    red spoked wheels ....$30 – 40
7. "Chocolat Menier," blue with black roof,
    silver spoked wheels ....$20 – 30
8. "Crawley Swapmeet," blue with
    black roof ....$275 – 325
9. "Dunlop," black with yellow roof ....$18 – 24
10. "EverReady," blue with white roof ...$18 – 24
11. "Frasers," blue with black roof ....$325 – 375
12. "Greenwich Appeal," yellow
    with black roof ....$275 – 325
13. "Ironbridge Museum," yellow
    with black roof ....$275 – 325
14. "Langendorf," yellow with black roof ..$40 – 60
15. "Lipton's," green with black roof,
    green spoked wheels ....$20 – 30
16. "Lipton's," green with black roof,
    silver spoked wheels ....$30 – 40
17. "Lyle's Golden," green with white roof ..$18 – 24
18. "Merita," yellow with black roof ....$40 – 60
19. "Nestle's," light blue with gray roof,
    red spoked wheels ....$20 – 30
20. "Nestle's Milk," blue with black roof $90 – 120
21. "Rose's Lime Juice," cream
    with black roof ....$18 – 24
22. "South Pacific Export Lager," YGB-10 ..$18 – 24
23. "Taystee," yellow with black roof,
    red disc wheels ....$30 – 40

24. "Taystee," yellow with black roof,
    red spoked wheels ....$14 – 18
25. "Wright's Coal Tar," brown with beige roof,
    silver or gold spoked wheels ......$14 – 18

Tank (see **Chieftain Tank, King Tiger Tank, M48A2 Tank, M551 Sheridan Tank, Crusader Tank,** etc.)

Tank Transporter (also see **Thornycroft Antar Tractor, Sanky 50-Ton Tank Transporter, Centurion Mk III Tank**)

Tank Transporter with M48A2 Tank, 10½", Battle Kings BK-106, 1974 . . . .$50 – 75

Tanker Truck (see **Peterbilt Tanker**)

Taylor Jumbo Crane, 5", King Size K-14, 1964 . .$50 – 70

The Londoner, 4¾", King Size K-15, 1973, doors on left side except where noted

1. beige, doors on right side, "Berlin ist eine Reise Wert!" . . . .$14 – 18
2. blue, "Alton Towers," UK issue . . . .$20 – 30
3. cream upper, blue lower, "Telegraph & Argus," UK issue . . . .$20 – 30
4. metallic silver, "Cada Toys," promotional . . . .$225 – 275
5. metallic silver, "London Dungeon" . . .$20 – 30
6. metallic silver, "Silver Jubilee 1952-1977," UK issue . . . .$20 – 30

7. metallic silver, "The Royal Wedding" . .$30 – 50
8. pale blue upper, white and dark blue lower, "1234-1984 Parish Church 750th Anniversary," UK issue . . . .$20 – 30
9. pale blue upper, white lower, "Macleans Toothpaste," UK issue . . . .$20 – 30
10. red, "Around London Tour Bus" . . . . .$10 – 12
11. red, "Besuchen Sie Berlin Haupstadt Der DDR," Germany issue . . . .$30 – 50
12. red, "Enter a Different World - Harrod's" . . . .$20 – 30
13. red, "Firestone" . . . .$20 – 30
14. red, "Hamley's" . . . .$20 – 30
15. red, "Harrod's for more than money can buy" . . . .$20 – 30
16. red, "London Dungeon" . . . .$16 – 20
17. red, "London Wide Tour Bus" . . . .$14 – 18
18. red, "Matchbox" on roof, Chinese pictograms on sides, China issue . .$300 – 500

19. red, "Nestle's Milkybar" . . . .$16 – 20
20. red, "Petticoat Lane" . . . .$14 – 18
21. red, "Swinging London Carnaby Street,"
    bell cast . . . .$30 – 50
22. red, "Swinging London Carnaby Street,"
    no bell cast . . . .$14 – 18
23. red, "The Planetarium" . . . .$14 – 18
24. red, "Tourist London – By Bus" . . . . . .$20 – 30
25. white upper, red lower,
    "Nestle's Milkybar" . . . .$16 – 20
26. yellow, "1234" with blue and red stripes on
    sides, "Save the Children" on roof, Live
    'N Learn / Matchbox Preschool . . . . .$8 – 10
27. yellow upper, brown lower, "London
    Wide Tour Bus" . . . .$14 – 18

Thomas Flyabout, 1909, Models of Yesteryear Y-12, introduced in 1967
    1. gold plated . . . .$50 – 60
    2. metallic bright blue with yellow
       seats and grille . . . .$900 – 1,000

3. **metallic bright blue with dark red
    seats and grille** . . . .$20 – 30
4. metallic fuchsia . . . .$20 – 30
5. metallic red . . . .$60 – 75
6. silver plated . . . .$50 – 60

**Thornycroft Antar Tractor, Sanky 50-Ton Tank
Transporter, Centurion Mk III Tank,
4½", Major Pack M-3, 1959** . . . .$150 – 200

Thunderclap, 4", King Size K-34, 1972
    1. black, "Matchbox 1" . . . .$14 – 18
    2. yellow, "Matchbox 34" . . . .$14 – 18

Tipper Truck (see **Scammell Tipper Truck**, also see **Dump Truck**)

Toyota 4x4 Hi-Lux, King Size K-171, 1989, Action Farming FM-4, 1991
    1. white . . . .$18 – 24
    2. red with milk cans and cow, FM-4 . . . . .$9 – 12

Tractor Transporter (see **Ford Tractor Transporter with three tractors**)

Tractor Transporter with two MB25 Mod Tractors, 6⅜", King Size K-21, 1974
    1. blue with yellow ramp . . . .$20 – 30

Transcontinental Double Freighter (see **Ford Transcontinental Double Freighter**)

Traxcavator Road Ripper (see **Caterpillar Traxcavator Road Ripper**)

Triumph Dolomite, 1939, The Dinky Collection DY-17, introduced in 1990
    1. red . . . .$20 – 30

Triumph Stag, 1969, The Dinky Collection DY-28, introduced in 1992
    1. dark green . . . .$18 – 24
    2. white . . . .$12 – 16

Triumph TR4A-IRS, 1965, The Dinky Collection DY-20, introduced in 1991
    1. white . . . .$12 – 16

Triumph TR8, DYB – 01, introduced in 1998
    1. dark green with brown roof . . . .$20 – 30

Troop Carrier with 226mm Howitzer, 8⅞", Battle Kings BK-116, 1977 . . . .$60 – 85

Tucker Torpedo, 1948, The Dinky Collection DY-11, introduced in 1990; DYG-06, introduced in 1996
    1. dark green, DYG-06 . . . .$18 – 24
    2. dark green, Matchbox Collectibles Oldies
       but Goodies I, issued 2004 . . . .$9 – 12
    3. metallic blue, DY-11 . . . .$18 – 24
    4. metallic red, DY-11 . . . .$18 – 24

5. **yellow, Matchbox Collectibles** . . . . . .$35 – 45

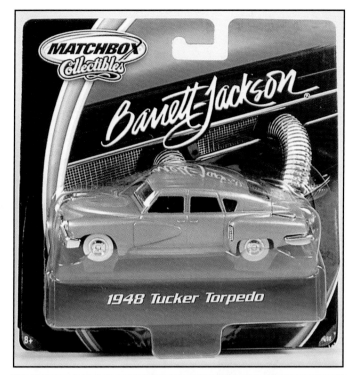

6. bronze, Barrett-Jackson Collection, 2003 .$10 – 14

U-Haul Truck (see **Ford Delivery Van**)

Unic Taxi, 1907, Models of Yesteryear Y-28, introduced in 1984
    1. blue . . . .$14 – 18

2. maroon . . . .$14 – 18

    3. white . . . .$14 – 18

Unimog (see **Mercedes Benz Unimog**)

Volkswagen Beetle, 1968; Matchbox Collectibles Budweiser Sports Cars DYM – 37622, introduced in 1999
    1. Bowling . . . .$30 – 40

Volkswagen Cabrio, 1949, VEM-01, introduced in 1997
    1. black . . . .$24 – 32

Volkswagen Deluxe Sedan, 1951, The Dinky Collection DY-6, introduced in 1989
    1. black . . . .$18 – 24
    2. pale blue . . . .$20 – 30
    3. red . . . .$18 – 24

Volkswagen Golf, King Size K-86, 1981
    1. black . . . .$9 – 12
    2. white . . . .$9 – 12
    3. yellow, "ADAC Straflenwacht,"
        Germany issue . . . .$30 – 40

Volkswagen Karmann Ghia, 1968, DY-35, introduced in 1995
    1. red . . . .$18 – 24

Volvo Ambulance, King Size K-96, 1984 . . . .$14 – 18

Volvo and Europa Caravelle Caravan, 10⅝", King Size K-69, 1980
    1. light brown Volvo, light yellow caravan . .$30 – 40
    2. red Volvo, white caravan . . . .$30 – 40

Volvo Estate Car, 5⅜", King Size K-74, 1980
    1. blue . . . .$14 – 18
    2. dark red . . . .$14 – 18
    3. light brown, part of K-69 . . . .$18 – 24
    4. red, part of K-69 . . . .$18 – 24

Volvo Rally Set, 10⅝", King Size K-76, 1981
    1. white Volvo, green Datsun . . . .$30 – 40

Walker Electric Van, 1919, Models of Yesteryear Y-29, introduced in 1985
    1. "Harrods Ltd.," olive . . . .$18 – 24
    2. "Harrod's Special Bread," olive . . . . . .$14 – 18
    3. "His Master's Voice," dark blue . . . . . .$14 – 18
    4. "Joseph Lucas," green . . . .$14 – 18

Wall's Ice Cream Truck (see **Bedford Ice Cream Truck**)

Waterous Fire Engine, 1906, 5", Matchbox
    Collectibles Fire Engine Collection

YFE-23, introduced in 1998 . . . .$35 – 50

Weatherill Hydraulic Excavator, 3¹¹⁄₁₆", King Size K-1, 1960 . . . .$100 – 125

Wells Fargo Stage Coach, Matchbox Collectibles "Historical Series" Collection YHS-03, introduced in 1993 . . . .$60 – 75

Wirlbelwind Flak PZ IV Tank, Matchbox Collectibles Great Tanks of World War II DYM-37582, issued 2000 . . . .$30 – 40

Wolesley Hornet, 1962, VEM-05, introduced in 1997

1. burgundy . . . .$24 – 32

Wreck Truck (see **Peterbilt Wreck Truck**)

Yorkshire Steam Wagon, 1917 Type WA, Models of Yesteryear Y-8, introduced in 1987; Y-32, introduced in 1990; Matchbox Collectibles "Great Beers of the World" Collection YGB-12, introduced in 1994; Matchbox Collectibles Age of Steam YAS-11, introduced in 1997

    1. "Fyffes," yellow, Y-8 . . . .$18 – 24
    2. "Great Western Railway Co.
       1087," YAS-11 . . . .$25 – 40
    3. "Johnny Walker Whisky," purple, Y-8 . .$18 – 24
    4. "Lowenbrau," YGB-12 . . . .$18 – 24
    5. "Samuel Smith," green, disassembled
       in framed display, Y-8 . . . .$125 – 150
    6. "Samuel Smith," purple, Y-32 . . . .$18 – 24
    7. "William Prichard Millennium Flour,"
       dark blue, Y-8 . . . .$18 – 24

ZakSpeed Ford Mustang, 5¹⁄₁₆", Specials SP7/8, 1984; Super Kings K-6, 1989; also issued as Super GT Sports, Turbo Specials, Muscle Cars, Alarm Cars, Graffic Traffic, LA Wheels

    1. black, "83," Specials SP8 . . . .$8 – 10
    2. black, "83," Turbo Specials TS2 . . . .$8 – 10
    3. blue, "QXR Duckhams," Specials SP7 . .$8 – 10
    4. blue, "QXR Duckhams," Super Kings K-6 .$8 – 10
    5. orange, blue and red, "20,"
       Super Kings K-1 . . . .$8 – 10
    6. orange with black stripes, Muscle Cars . .$8 – 10

    7. pearl white, "Motul 28," Specials SP8 . .$8 – 10
    8. white, "Ford 16," Specials SP7 . . . .$8 – 10
    9. white with blue stripes, Muscle Cars . . .$8 – 10
    10. yellow, blue and red, "20," Turbo
       Specials TS2 . . . .$8 – 10

155mm Self Propelled Howitzer (see **Self Propelled 155mm Howitzer**)

Part 2: Two Packs, Twin Packs, Trailers, Matchmates, 900 Series Long Haul (TP-), Convoy, Super Rigs (CY-), Highway Express (HE-)

Variously sold as Two Packs, Twin Packs or Trailers, this series is defined by its packaging, a vehicle usually accompanied by a trailer. Some of these trailers were never sold separately. One such trailer available only as part of a set is the Glider Trailer, which included TP-7 in 1977, TP-102 in 1984, TP-118 in 1987, and TP-122 in 1989. These sets first appeared in the 1976 catalog, although packages of two complementary models were available as early as 1968 with models such as #1 Mercedes Benz Lorry and matching #2 Mercedes Benz Trailer. The pair was reintroduced as TP-1 in 1976 with Superfast wheels. Since most models in this series are available separately, values listed are for sets in their original containers. The information in parentheses indicates the model number and year each vehicle was introduced.

1982 saw the introduction of the new Convoy series, derived from the semi tractor/trailers from the Twin Pack / 900 Long Haul Series of the previous year (see Twin Pack listing). The Convoy series designation was changed to HE for Highway Express in 1983 and changed back to Convoy the following year. When Tyco purchased Matchbox in 1992, they changed the name again to Super Rigs.

All models are approximately 7½" long. When White Rose Collectibles started a cooperative marketing effort with Matchbox, it produced a series of racing transporters based on Convoy models, called Superstar Transporters.

Note: The abbreviation "C.O.E." stands for "Cab Over Engine."

Aircraft Transporter, DAF, Convoy CY-21, 1987; CY-108, 1992
1. black, "AC102," CY-21 . . . .$30 – 35
2. red cab, carriage and trailer base with SB-37 Hawk, CY-108 . . . .$9 – 12
3. white, "Airtrainer," CY-21 . . . .$10 – 12
4. white, "Red Rebels," CY-21 . . . .$7 – 9
5. white, no markings, Graffic Traffic . . . .$12 – 15
6. white, Aerobatic Team," "Flying Aces," CY-21 . . . .$12 – 15

Aircraft Transporter, Kenworth C.O.E., Convoy CY-12, 1984
1. white cab with blue and dark green tampos, blue plane, "DARTS," England cast . .$12 – 15
2. white cab with blue and brown tampos, blue plane, "DARTS," England cast . . . . . .$12 – 15
3. white cab with two-tone blue tampos, blue plane, "DARTS," Macau cast . . . .$10 – 12

Aircraft Transporter, Mack, Convoy CY-29, 1991
1. red with red plane, "RED REBELS" tampo . .$4 – 5

Alvis Stalwart and Dodge Wrecker (see **Military Alvis Stalwart and Dodge Wrecker**)

Ambulance and Fire Chief, TP-10, 1978 (see **Fire Chief and Ambulance**)

Articulated Dump Truck (also see **Articulated Tipper**)

Articulated Dump Truck, Kenworth C.O.E. Aerodyne, Convoy CY-20, 1987
1. yellow, "TAYLOR WOODROW" . . . .$7 – 9
2. red with yellow trailer, red design . . . . .$4 – 6
3. yellow, "EUROBRAN" . . . .$7 – 9
4. yellow with black and white road design . .$7 – 9

Articulated Dump Truck, Scania T142, Convoy CY-20, 1987
1. pink, "READYMIX" . . . .$16 – 20

Articulated Petrol Tanker and Trailer, TP-2, 1976
1. green windows, red cab and trailer, white tank, "Exxon" labels . . . .$14 – 18
2. amber windows, red cab and trailer, white tank, "Exxon" labels . . . .$14 – 18

Articulated Tipper, Peterbilt, Convoy CY-106, 1990, Australia
1. pink cab, gray dumper with black base, "Readymix" . . . .$14 – 16

Articulated Truck (#50, 1973) and Trailer (#50, 1980), TP-16, 1980
1. yellow cab, blue dumper, trailer with blue dumper . . . .$14 – 18
2. red cab, metallic gray dumper, trailer with metallic gray dumper . . . .$24 – 32

BMW 323i Cabriolet (#39, 1985) and Caravan (#31, 1977), TP-123, 1989
1. metallic silver blue with dark blue stripe, gray caravan with orange stripe . . . .$9 – 12
2. white with geometric design, white caravan with matching design . . . .$9 – 12

BMW 323i Cabriolet (#39, 1985) and Glider Trailer, TP-118, 1987
1. red with "Gliding Club," red glider trailer with "Auto Glide" . . . .$14 – 18

BMW 323i Cabriolet (#39, 1985) and Inflatable Raft, TP-127, 1991

1. white with red and blue design, dark blue raft with gray hull, white trailer with red and blue design . . . .$9 – 12

Boat Transporter, TP-26, 1979 (see **Long Haul Boat Transporter**)

Boat Transporter, Kenworth Conventional Sleeper Cab, Convoy CY-4, 1982; HE-2, 1983
1. orange cab, boat with orange hull, green windows . . . .$10 – 12
2. orange cab, boat with orange hull, red windows . . . .$10 – 12
3. orange cab, boat with orange hull, clear windows . . . .$10 – 12

Bomag Road Roller (#72, 1979; #40, 1991; #68, 1992) and Faun Mobile Crane (#42, 1985-1997), CS-83, 1992
1. yellow road roller, yellow crane with red cab, plastic accessories . . . .$7 – 9

Box Car, Kenworth Conventional, Convoy CY-36, 1992
1. white, "Charitoys" labels . . . .$30 – 35

2. **orange cab, black container, "TRICK TRUCKIN"** . . . .$4 – 5
3. fluorescent orange, yellow container, "MATCHBOX - GET IN THE FAST LANE" . .$4 – 5

Box Car, Peterbilt, Convoy CY-19, 1987
1. white, "ANSETT WRIDGWAYS" . . . .$16 – 20

Box Container Truck, TP-24, 1979 (see **Long Haul Box Container Truck**)

Box Truck, DAF, Convoy CY-9, 1982; HE-9, 1982; TP-24, 1982; CY-24, 1988
1. yellow cab and container, Macau cast, "IPEC" . . . .$12 – 15
2. red, "FERRARI" . . . .$7 – 9
3. blue, "PICKFORDS" . . . .$12 – 15
4. white, "PORSCHE" . . . .$7 – 9
5. white, "CIRCUS CIRCUS" . . . .$7 – 9
6. white, "SAUDIA" . . . .$60 – 75
7. blue, "MITRE 10 RACING" . . . .$10 – 12

8. white, black container, "BASSETT'S LIQUORICE ALLSORTS" . . . .$10 – 12
9. white, yellow container, "BASSETT'S JELLY BABIES" . . . .$10 – 12
10. dark green, "JAGUAR" . . . .$7 – 9
11. orange and red, "PARCEL POST" . . . .$10 – 12
12. white, "RENAULT ELF," "CANON WILLIAMS" . . . .$10 – 12

Box Truck, Ford Aeromax, CY-39 Convoy, 1994; CY-39 Super Rigs, 1995

1. **blue, "Hawaiian Punch"** . . . .$7 – 9

2. **light orange, "Honey Nut Cheerios"** . . . . .$7 – 9
3. red, "Heinz Tomato Ketchup Squeezable!" . . . .$7 – 9
4. white, "Pepsi," "Diet Pepsi" . . . .$4 – 5
5. yellow, "Cheerios" . . . .$4 – 5

Box Truck, Kenworth Conventional Aerodyne, Convoy CY-8, 1982; HE-8, 1983; Convoy CY-9, 1982; HE-9, 1982; TP-24, 1982; Super Rigs, 1995
1. red, red container with white roof, black doors, England cast, "REDCAP" . . . .$40 – 50
2. red, red container with black roof and doors, England cast, "REDCAP" . . . .$80 – 100
3. red, red container with black roof, white doors, England cast, "REDCAP" . . .$80 – 100

4. **red, "Skittles"** . . . .$9 – 12

5. black cab, black container, England cast, "MIDNIGHT X-PRESS" . . . .$10 – 12

6. black cab, black container, Macau cast, "MIDNIGHT X-PRESS" . . . .$7 – 9

7. black cab, black container, Macau, "MOVING IN NEW DIRECTIONS" . .$150 – 175

8. black cab, black container, Macau, "MOVING IN NEW DIRECTIONS," "Personal Contact is Barry Oxford" on roof . .$275 – 300

9. black cab, black container, Macau, "MOVING IN NEW DIRECTIONS," "Personal Contact is Anita Jones" on roof . .$275 – 300

10. black cab, black container, Macau, "MOVING IN NEW DIRECTIONS," "Personal Contact is Keith Mottram" on roof . .$275 – 300

11. black cab, black container, Macau, "MOVING IN NEW DIRECTIONS," "Personal Contact is Terry Blyton" on roof . . .$275 – 300

12. black cab, black container, Macau, "MOVING IN NEW DIRECTIONS," "Personal Contact is Jenny Brindley" on roof . .$275 – 300

13. black cab and container, Macau cast, "STANLEY" . . . .$12 – 15

14. orange, "Reese's" . . . .$9 – 12

15. white cab and container, Macau cast, "PAUL ARPIN VAN LINES" . . . .$12 – 15

16. white cab, container, "Matchbox Compliments Macau Die – Cast Co. Ltd." . . . .$800 – 1,000

17. white cab and container, "PAUL ARPIN VAN LINES" with "NFL" logo . . . .$12 – 18

18. white, "Matchbox — In Celebration of Universal Group's 20th Anniversary" . . . .$1,250 – 1,500

19. white cab and container, Macau cast, "Canadian Tire" . . . . . .$12 – 15

20. white cab and container, Macau, "Merry Christmas 1988 MICA Members" . . . .$20 – 25

21. blue cab and container, Macau cast, "Mitre 10" . . . .$12 – 15

22. blue cab and container, Macau cast, "Spaulding" . . . .$30 – 40

23. white cab and container, Macau, "Merry Christmas MICA Members 1990" . . . .$20 – 25

24. black cab and container, Thailand cast, "MIDNIGHT X-PRESS" . . . .$4 – 5

25. black cab and container, Thailand cast, "COOL PAINT CO." . . . .$4 – 5

26. white cab and container, "HERSHEY'S" . .$4 – 5

27. white cab and container, "TRUCKIN' USA" . .$4 – 5

Box Truck, Kenworth C.O.E. Aerodyne, Convoy CY-8, 1982; HE-8, 1983; Convoy CY-9, 1982; HE-9, 1982; TP-24, 1982

1. black with "Harley-Davidson" tampos, Macau cast . . . .$7 – 9

2. black cab, black container, England cast, "MIDNIGHT X-PRESS" . . . .$40 – 50

3. red cab, white container, "Pizza Hut" . . . .$9 – 12

4. red cab and container, "NINTENDO," Thailand cast . . . .$4 – 5

5. silver-gray, blue roof, doors, Macau, "MATCHBOX SHOWLINER" . . . .$325 – 375

6. white, "KFC" . . . .$7 – 9

7. white, England cast, "MATCHBOX" . . .$60 – 75

8. white, England cast, "REDCAP" . . . . . .$40 – 50

9. white, red container, white roof and doors, "SKI FRUIT YOGURT" . . . .$80 – 100

10. white, red container, white roof, red doors, England cast, "REDCAP" . . . .$40 – 50

11. white, white container, roof and doors, Macau, "K-Line" . . . .$300 – 400

12. white cab, container, roof and doors, Macau cast, "MATCHBOX" . . . .$12 – 15

13. white, Macau cast, "Matchbox," "This Truck Delivers 1988" . . . .$40 – 50

14. white, Macau cast, "Matchbox," "This Truck Delivers 1989" . . . .$200 – 250

15. white with red container, roof and doors, Macau cast, "K-Line" . . . .$175 – 225

Box Truck, Mack Convoy CY-27, 1989
1. white, "A GREAT NAME IN TRUCKS - MACK" . . . .$12 – 15
2. chrome, black container, "Celebrating a Decade of Matchbox Conventions 1991" . . . .$30 – 40

Box Truck, Scania, Convoy CY-4, 1985, Australia; Convoy CY-16, 1985
1. white cab, and container, black trailer, "Ansett" labels, Australia . . . .$12 – 15
2. white with "7-Up" labels . . . .$12 – 15
3. white with upside-down "7-Up" labels . .$30 – 35
4. white with dark blue container, "DUCKHAM'S" . . . .$12 – 15
5. purple with purple trailer, "EDWIN SHIRLEY" . . . .$12 – 15
6. white with "WIMPEY" tampo . . . .$12 – 15
7. white with "SIGNAL TOOTHPASTE" . . .$12 – 15
8. white with red container, "HEINZ TOMATO KETCHUP SQUEEZABLE" . . . .$12 – 15
9. yellow with white container, "WEETABIX" . . . .$12 – 15
10. blue, "MATEY BUBBLE BATH" . . . .$12 – 15
11. white, "GOLDEN WONDER POTATO CRISPS" . . . .$12 – 15
12. white, "MERCHANT TIRE & AUTO CENTERS" . . . .$12 – 15
13. white, "Merry Christmas 1988 MICA Members" . . . .$25 – 30
14. yellow, "WEETABIX" . . . .$12 – 15
15. purple, "RIBENA" . . . .$12 – 15
16. white, "Merry Christmas 1989 MICA Members" . . . .$30 – 35
17. white, "GOODYEAR VECTOR" . . . .$7 – 9
18. white, "SAUDIA" . . . .$60 – 75
19. red with white trailer, "KENTUCKY FRIED CHICKEN" . . . .$12 – 15

Breakdown Set, TP-6, 1976 – Variations:
Toe Joe (#74, 1972), and Racing Mini (#29, 1970)
1. red Toe Joe with green booms, orange Racing Mini with "29" labels . . . . .$250 – 300
2. red Toe Joe with red booms, orange Racing Mini with "29" labels . . . .$250 – 300
3. yellow Toe Joe with red booms, orange Racing Mini with "29" labels . . . .$14 – 18
4. yellow Toe Joe with green booms, orange Racing Mini with "29" labels . . . .$14 – 18
5. green Toe Joe with green booms, orange Racing Mini with "29" labels . . . .$14 – 18
6. green Toe Joe with green booms, orange Racing Mini with "3" labels . . . .$16 – 20

Toe Joe (#74, 1972), and Range Rover Police Patrol (#20, 1975)
7. yellow Toe Joe with red booms, orange Police Patrol with "Site Engineer" labels . . . .$30 – 40
8. green Toe Joe with green booms, orange Police Patrol with "Site Engineer" labels . . . .$30 – 40
9. green Toe Joe with white booms, orange Police Patrol with "Site Engineer" labels . .$250 – 300

Toe Joe (#74, 1972), and Volkswagen 1500 (#15, 1968)
10. red Toe Joe with red booms, white Volkswagen with "137" labels . . . .$250 – 300
11. yellow Toe Joe with red booms, white Volkswagen with "137" labels . . . . . .$36 – 48

Toe Joe (#74, 1972), and Saab Sonnet (#65, 1973)
12. yellow Toe Joe with red booms, metallic blue Saab . . . .$36 – 54

Ford Wrecker (#61, 1978), and Racing Mini (#29, 1970)
13. red wrecker with white booms, orange Racing Mini with "29" labels . . . .$14 – 18
14. red wrecker with white booms and "24 Hour," orange Racing Mini with no labels . .$14 – 18
15. red wrecker with red booms, orange Racing Mini with "3" labels . . . .$16 – 20
16. red wrecker with green booms, orange Racing Mini with "29" labels . . . . . .$250 – 300
17. yellow wrecker with red booms, orange Racing Mini with "29" labels . . . .$14 – 18

Car Transporter, Kenworth C.O.E., Convoy CY-1, 1982; HE-1, 1983
1. red cab, red trailer with beige ramp and white stripes . . . .$10 – 12
2. red cab with "4" label on roof, red trailer with beige ramp and no stripes . . . .$175 – 200
3. red cab with no label on roof, red trailer with beige ramp and no stripes . . . .$10 – 12
4. yellow cab, dark blue trailer, yellow ramp . . . .$6 – 9
5. blue cab, blue trailer, yellow ramp . . . .$4 – 6

Caterpillar Bulldozer (#64, 1979) and Tractor Shovel (#29, 1976-1997), CS-81, 1992
1. yellow bulldozer with red roof, yellow tractor shovel with red shovel, plastic accessories . . . .$7 – 9

Cattle Truck and Trailer, TP-19, 1979; TP-103, 1984 (see **Dodge Stake Truck and Trailer**)

Circus Set, TP-128, 1992 – Variations:
Volvo Covered Truck (#23, 1985; #20, 1986; #62, 1990) and Trailer (#2, 1968)
1. red with white canopies, "Big Top Circus" . . . .$16 – 20

Dodge Truck (Zoo Truck #72, 1992 with container replacing cage) and Trailer (#2, 1968)
2. red truck with white container, red trailer with white canopy, "Big Top Circus" . .$14 – 18

Citroen CX Station Wagon (#12, 1979) and Boat (#9, 1966), TP-109, 1984
1. white Citroen with "Marine," boat has blue deck, white hull, no label, blue trailer . .$16 – 20
2. white Citroen with "Marine," boat has blue deck, white hull, "8" label, blue trailer . .$16 – 20
3. white Citroen with "Marine," boat has white deck, blue hull, "8" label, blue trailer . .$16 – 20
4. white Citroen with "Marine," boat has white deck, blue hull, "8" label, orange trailer . . . .$16 – 20
5. white Citroen with "Marine," boat has white deck, blue hull, no label, orange trailer . . . .$30 – 40
6. white Citroen with "Ambulance," boat has white deck, blue hull, "8" label, orange trailer . . . .$16 – 20
7. white Citroen with "Ambulance," boat has white deck, white hull, "8" label, orange trailer . . . .$16 – 20

Citroen and Motorcycle Trailer with three plastic motorcycles, TP-21, 1979 (see **Motorcycle Set**)

Citroen Matchmates, M-01, 1984
1. white Citroen CX Station Wagon (#12, 1979) with "Marine," black Citroen 15CV (#44, 1983) . . . .$14 – 18

Construction Low Loader, Convoy CY-203, 1989
1. yellow, with Atlas Excavator . . . .$10 – 12

Container Truck, DAF, Convoy CY-25, 1989
1. yellow, "IPEC" . . . .$12 – 15
2. blue, "CROOKES HEALTHCARE" . . . . .$12 – 15
3. white and orange, "UNIGATE" . . . . . .$12 – 15
4. red, "ROYAL MAIL PARCELS" . . . . . .$12 – 15
5. blue, "COMMA PERFORMANCE OIL" . .$12 – 15
6. white, "LEISURE WORLD" . . . .$12 – 15
7. white, "PEPSI TEAM SUZUKI" . . . .$12 – 15
8. white and orange, "TNT IPEC" . . . . .$10 – 12
9. white, "PIONEER" . . . .$12 – 15
10. metallic gold cab, black container, "DURACELL" . . . .$12 – 15
11. yellow, "ZWEIFEL POMY CHIPS" . . . . .$12 – 15
12. green, "M" and orange stripe . . . .$12 – 15
13. white, "TOBLERONE" . . . .$10 – 12
14. white, "PIRELLI GRIPPING STUFF" . . . .$10 – 12
15. white, "XP" . . . .$10 – 12
16. white, "HB RACING" . . . .$10 – 12
17. white, "GARDEN FESTIVAL WALES" . . .$12 – 15
18. brown, light gray container, "UNITED PARCEL SERVICE" . . . .$20 – 25

Container Truck, Ford Aeromax, Convoy CY-37, 1993
1. yellow, "Radical Cams" . . . .$4 – 5

Container Truck, Kenworth, Convoy CY-38, 1993
1. black, "Matchbox Racing 5" . . . .$4 – 5

Container Truck, Mack, Convoy CY-28, 1989
1. white with white containers, "BIG TOP CIRCUS" . . . .$12 – 15
2. white, "DHL Worldwide Express" . . . . .$7 – 9
3. red with white containers, "BIG TOP CIRCUS" . . . .$4 – 6

Container Truck, Scania, Convoy CY-18, 1986
1. blue cab with black interior, "VARTA BATTERIES" . . . .$35 – 40
2. blue cab with gray interior, "VARTA BATTERIES" . . . .$12 – 15
3. white, "WALL'S ICE CREAM" . . . .$12 – 15
4. red, "KIT KAT" . . . .$12 – 15
5. orange, "BREAKAWAY" . . . .$12 – 15
6. white, "7- UP" . . . .$12 – 15

Corvette Matchmates, M-03, 1984
1. red 1984 Corvette Convertible (#14, 1983; #69, 1983; #28, 1990) and metallic silver pearl Corvette (#62, 1979; #21, 1983) . .$14 – 18

Cougar (see **Mercury Cougar**)

Cougar Dragster (see **Mercury Cougar Dragster**)

Covered Container Truck, TP-23, 1979 (see **Long Haul Covered Container Truck**)

Covered Truck, Kenworth Conventional Aerodyne, Convoy CY-5, 1982; HE-5, 1982; TP-23, 1982
1. white cab, white trailer with green cover, "INTERSTATE TRUCKING" . . . .$8 – 12
2. green cab, white trailer, England cast "INTERSTATE TRUCKING" . . . .$15 – 20

Covered Truck, Peterbilt Conventional Aerodyne, Convoy CY-5, 1982; HE-5, 1982; TP-23, 1982
1. green cab, white trailer, Macau cast, "INTERSTATE TRUCKING" labels . . . . . .$12 – 15
2. yellow cab, silver trailer with yellow cover, "MICHELIN" tampo . . . .$10 – 12
3. orange, Macau cast, "WALT'S FARM FRESH PRODUCE" . . . .$7 – 9
4. orange, Thailand cast, "WALT'S FARM FRESH PRODUCE" . . . .$4 – 6

Covered Truck, Scania, Convoy CY-23, 1988
1. yellow, "MICHELIN" . . . .$10 – 12

DAF Road Train, King Size K-122, 1986
1. white, "Eurotrans" . . . .$20 – 30
2. white, "Toblerone" . . . .$20 – 30

Datsun 260Z 2+2 (#67, 1978) and Caravan (#31, 1977), TP-107, 1984
1. metallic gray Datsun with two-tone stripes, white Caravan with "Mobile 500" . . .$14 – 18

Diesel Shunter (#24, 1978) and Side Tipper, TP-20, 1979, TP-125, 1991
1. yellow Shunter, yellow Side Tipper with red dumper, England cast, TP-20, 1979 . .$14 – 18
2. yellow Shunter, yellow Side Tipper with black dumper, England cast, TP-20, 1979 . .$16 – 20
3. yellow Shunter, yellow Side Tipper with red dumper, China cast, TP-125 . . . .$9 – 12

Dodge Stake Truck (#4, 1967-1970; issued as Dodge Cattle Truck #71, 1976-1991) and Trailer, TP-19, 1979; TP-103, 1984
1. red with beige stakes, black cows, TP-19 . . . .$14 – 18
2. red with beige stakes, brown cows, TP-19 . . . .$14 – 18
3. red with beige stakes, brown cows, TP-103 . . . .$9 – 12
4. red with orange stakes, dark brown cows, TP-19 . . . .$16 – 20
5. yellow with light brown stakes, reddish brown cows, TP-103 . . . .$9 – 12
6. pale blue with light brown stakes, black cows, TP-103 . . . .$9 – 12
7. green with yellow stakes, black cows, TP-103 . . . .$8 – 10

Double Container Truck, TP-22, 1979 (see **Long Haul Double Container Truck**)

Double Container Truck, DAF, Convoy CY-26, 1989
1. light blue with dark blue containers, "P & O" . . . .$12 – 15

Double Container Truck, Ford Aeromax, Convoy CY-111, 1993 from White Rose Collectibles
1. black, "Charitoys 1993" . . . .$35 – 40

Double Container Truck, Kenworth Conventional Aerodyne, Convoy CY-3, 1982; HE-3, 1982; TP-22
1. red cab, black trailer, "UNIROYAL" labels . . . .$10 – 12
2. white cab, black trailer, "FEDERAL EXPRESS" . . . .$10 – 12

Double Container Truck, Peterbilt Conventional Aerodyne, Convoy CY-3, 1982; HE-3, 1982; TP-22, 1982
1. red cab, black trailer, "UNIROYAL" labels . . . .$10 – 12
2. red cab, white trailer, "UNIROYAL" labels . . . .$16 – 20
3. red cab, yellow trailer, "LINFOX" tampo . . . .$12 – 15

Double Tanker Set (Freeway Gas Tanker #63, 1973, and Freeway Gas Tanker Trailer, #63, 1978), TP-17, 1979
1. red cab/white trailer with "Burmah" labels, red and white tanker trailer with "Burmah" labels . . . .$14 – 18
2. red cab/white trailer with "Chevron" labels, red and white tanker trailer with "Burmah" labels . . . .$14 – 18
3. red cab/red trailer with "Chevron" labels, red and white tanker trailer with "Chevron" labels . . . .$14 – 18
4. red cab/white trailer with "Exxon" labels, white tanker trailer with "Exxon" labels . .$120 – 160
5. white cab/yellow trailer with "Shell" labels, yellow and white tanker trailer with "Shell" labels . . . .$14 – 18
6. white cab/white trailer with "Exxon" labels, white tanker trailer with "Exxon" labels . .$14 – 18
7. white cab/yellow trailer with "Exxon" labels, yellow and white tanker trailer with "Exxon" labels . . . .$30 – 40
8. white cab/green trailer with "BP" labels, white and green tanker trailer with "BP" labels . . . .$24 – 36

Emergency Center, Peterbilt, Convoy CY-34, 1992
1. fluorescent orange . . . .$6 – 9

Emergency Set, TP-7, 1976 – Variations:
Stretcha Fetcha (#46, 1972) and Mercury Fire Chief (#59, 1971)
1. white Stretcha Fetcha, white Mercury Fire Chief . . . .$14 – 18
Stretcha Fetcha (#46, 1972) and Fire Chief (#64, 1976)
2. white Stretcha Fetcha, red Fire Chief . .$14 – 18

Farming Twin Pack, FM-100, 1993
1. Mercedes Benz Trac 1600 Turbo Farm Tractor (#73, 1990) and Seeder (#712, 1993) . . .$5 – 7
2. Mercedes Benz Trac 1600 Turbo Farm Tractor (#73, 1990) and Farm Trailer (#711, 1993) . .$5 – 7
3. Tractor Shovel (#29, 1976-1997; #237, 1993; #13) and Tipping Trailer (#710, 1993) . . .$5 – 7
4. Ford Tractor (#236, 1993) and Farm Trailer (#711, 1993) . . . .$5 – 7

5. Ford Tractor (#236, 1993) and Rotovator
    (#713, 1993) . . . .$5 – 7

Field Car (#18, 1969) and Honda Motorcycle Trailer
(#38, 1967), TP-8, 1977
1. dark orange Field Car with no labels, orange
    trailer with "Honda" labels . . . .$16 – 20
2. dark orange Field Car with "179," orange
    trailer with no labels . . . .$20 – 25
3. orange Field Car with checkerboard label,
    orange trailer with "Honda" labels . .$14 – 18
4. orange Field Car with checkerboard label,
    orange trailer with no labels . . . .$14 – 18
5. yellow Field Car with checkerboard label,
    orange trailer with no labels . . . .$14 – 18
6. yellow Field Car with checkerboard label,
    yellow trailer with "Honda" labels . . .$14 – 18
7. yellow Field Car with checkerboard label,
    yellow trailer with no labels . . . .$14 – 18
8. white Field Car with checkerboard label,
    orange trailer with "Honda" labels . .$500 – 700

Field Car (#18, 1969) and Team Matchbox Racer
(#24, 1973), TP-9, 1978
1. red Field Car with "44" label, red Team Racer
    with "44" label . . . .$14 – 18
2. orange Field Car with "44" label, orange
    Team Racer with "44" label . . . .$80 – 120
3. orange Field Car with checkerboard label,
    orange Team Racer with "44" label . .$80 – 120

Field Car and Volkswagen Van (see **Military Field Car
and Volkswagen Van**)

Fire Chief and Ambulance, TP-10, 1978 – Variations:
Fire Chief (#64, 1976) and Mercedes Benz Ambulance (#3, 1968)
1. red Fire Chief, white ambulance . . .$14 – 18
Mercury Park Lane Fire Chief (#59, 1971) and Mercedes Benz Ambulance (#3, 1968)
2. red Mercury Fire Chief,
    white ambulance . . . .$14 – 18

Fire Engine, Kenworth C.O.E. Aerodyne, Convoy CY-
13, 1984
1. red with "DENVER" label, white "8,"
    "FIRE DEPT," England . . . .$600 – 750

Fire Engine, Peterbilt Conventional, Convoy CY-13, 1984
1. red with white "8" and "FIRE DEPT," white
    ladder, England cast . . . .$15 – 20

Fire Engine, Peterbilt custom cab with roof lights,
Convoy CY-13, 1984
1. red with "8" and "FIRE DEPT,"
    Macau cast . . . .$10 – 12

2. red with "8" and "FIRE DEPT,"
    Thailand cast . . . .$4 – 5
3. fluorescent orange, "CITY FIRE
    DEPT 15," Thailand . . . .$4 – 6

Flareside Pickup and Seafire Boat (see **Ford Flareside
Pickup and Seafire Boat**)

Ford Cortina 1600 GL (#55, 1979) and Pony Trailer
(#43, 1968), TP-111, 1984
1. metallic red Ford Cortina with black
    stripe, beige Pony Trailer with silver
    horseshoes design . . . .$9 – 12
2. metallic tan Ford Cortina with black stripe,
    beige Pony Trailer with horsehead label . .$9 – 12

Ford Escort RS2000 (#9, 1978) and Boat (#9, 1966), TP-
109, 1984
1. dark green Escort with seagull labels, boat
has white deck, blue hull, "8," orange trailer . .$60 – 80

Ford Escort XR3i (#17, 1985) and Boat (#9, 1966), TP-
115, 1987
1. white Ford Escort with "XR3i," white boat
    with "Seaspray," black trailer . . . .$9 – 12
2. metallic blue Ford Escort with spatter
    design, blue boat with spatter design,
    black trailer . . . .$9 – 12

Ford Escort XR3i (#17, 1985) and Glider Trailer, TP-
102, 1984
1. light green Ford Escort, dark green trailer with
    seagull labels . . . .$16 – 20
2. dark green Ford Escort, dark green trailer
    with seagull labels . . . .$9 – 12

Ford Flareside Pickup (#53, 1982) and Seafire Boat
(#5, 1975), TP-119, 1987
1. yellow pickup with "Ford," yellow Seafire
    with blue hull, "460" . . . .$9 – 12

Ford Matchmates, M-02, 1984
1. white, red and blue Ford Model A Van (#38,
    1982-1997) with "Pepsi," tan and brown Ford
    Model A (#73, 1979; #55, 1991) . . . . .$14 – 18

Ford Tractor (#46, 1978) **and Hay Trailer** (#40, 1967),
TP-11, 1979
1. blue tractor, yellow hay trailer with
    no stakes . . . .$16 – 20
2. blue tractor, blue hay trailer with
    black stakes . . . .$16 – 20
3. blue tractor, beige hay trailer
    with black stakes . . . .$180 – 220
4. lime green tractor, beige hay trailer
    with black stakes . . . .$180 – 220

5. lime green tractor, red hay trailer
with black stakes . . . . $16 – 20

Ford Tractor (#46, 1978) and Hay Trailer (#40, 1967),
TP-108, 1984
1. blue tractor, red hay trailer . . . . $9 – 12
2. yellow tractor, yellow hay trailer . . . . . $9 – 12
3. green tractor, yellow hay trailer . . . . . . $9 – 12

Freeway Gas Tanker and Tanker Trailer (see **Double Tanker Set**)

Gas Tanker (also see **Double Tanker Set, Petrol Tanker, Tanker**)

Gas Tanker, Ford Aeromax, Convoy CY-7, 1999
1. bright blue cab, chrome tank, "Exxon,"
Premiere Collection . . . . $12 – 15

Gas Tanker, Kenworth, Convoy CY-105, 1989
1. white with gold and black stripes . . . $12 – 15
2. white with "Shell" tampo . . . . $12 – 15

Glider Set, TP-7, 1977 – Variations:
Field Car (#18, 1969) with glider and trailer
1. yellow Field Car with checkerboard
label, yellow trailer with "Gliding
Club" labels . . . . $40 – 50
Ford Escort (#9, 1978) with glider and trailer
2. green Ford with seagull labels, green trailer
with seagull labels . . . . $9 – 12
Jeep (#38, 1976) with glider and trailer
3. red Jeep with black base, red trailer with
"Gliding Club" labels . . . . $900 – 1,200
4. yellow Jeep with black base, yellow trailer
with "Gliding Club" labels . . . . $14 – 18
5. yellow Jeep with white base, yellow trailer
with "Gliding Club" labels . . . . $14 – 18
6. yellow Jeep with white base, yellow trailer
with no labels . . . . $14 – 18

Graffic Traffic Metal Flakes, 1994
1. Ford Thunderbird (# 7, 1993) and Lamborghini
Countach (#67, 1985 – 1997) . . . . $6 – 8
2. Chevrolet Lumina (#54, 1990; #267, 1994) and
Sauber Group C Racer (#46/#66, 1985) . . $6 – 8

Grove Crane, Convoy CY-30, 1992
1. orange-yellow, red crane cab, yellow
boom, "AT1100 Grove" . . . . $6 – 9

Helicopter Transporter, Kenworth C.O.E., HE-11, 1983;
Convoy CY-11, 1984 – Includes 75-F Helicopter with
pilot and large windows
1. silver-gray cab, "ACE HIRE," 75-F in silver-gray
with "600," England cast . . . . $10 – 12

2. silver-gray cab, "ACE HIRE," 75-F in pearl
silver with "600," Macau cast . . . . $7 – 9
3. black cab, "AIR CAR," 75-F in black with
"AIR CAR," Macau cast . . . . $7 – 9
4. dark blue cab, 75-F in white with
"RESCUE," Macau cast . . . . $10 – 12
5. black cab, "AIR CAR," 75-F in black with
"AIR CAR," Thailand cast . . . . $4 – 5

Helicopter Transporter, Mack, Convoy CY-33, 1992
1. white with Mission Chopper . . . . $6 – 9
2. white with Mission
Chopper, "Rijkspolitie" . . . . $20 – 25

Highway Tanker and Trailer (see **Double Tanker Set**)

Holiday Set, TP-4, 1976 – Variations: AMX Javelin (#9,
1972) and Eccles Caravan (#57, 1970)
1. lime green Javelin (doors open), yellow
caravan with flower and stripe label . . $14 – 18
2. dark green Javelin (doors cast shut), yellow
caravan with flower and stripe label . . $14 – 18
3. metallic blue Javelin (doors cast shut), yellow
caravan with flower and stripe label . . $14 – 18
Datsun 260Z (#67, 1978) and Eccles Caravan (#57,
1970)
4. blue Datsun, yellow caravan with flower
and stripe label . . . . $40 – 50
Ford Capri (#54, 1971) and Eccles Caravan (#57,
1970), 1976
5. orange Ford, cream caravan with
flower and stripe label . . . . $20 – 30
Maserati Bora (#32, 1972) and Eccles Caravan (#57,
1970)
6. metallic gold Maserati, beige caravan
with flower and stripe label . . . . $30 – 40
7. metallic gold Maserati, beige caravan
with dots label . . . . $30 – 40
8. metallic gold Maserati, beige caravan
with seagull label . . . . $30 – 40
Renault 5TL (#21, 1978) and Eccles Caravan (#57,
1970)
9. blue Renault, yellow caravan with
flower and stripe label . . . . $40 – 50
Vauxhall Guildsman (#40, 1971) and Eccles Caravan
(#57, 1970)
10. red Guildsman with label, yellow caravan
with flower and stripe label . . . . $20 – 30
11. red Guildsman with label, yellow caravan
with dots label . . . . $20 – 30
12. red Guildsman with label, yellow caravan
with no label . . . . $20 – 30
13. red Guildsman with printed design, yellow
caravan with flower and stripe label . . $20 – 30
14. red Guildsman with no label, white caravan
with seagull label . . . . $30 – 40

15. pink Guildsman with label, yellow caravan
with flower and stripe label ....$30 – 40
Volkswagen Golf (#7, 1976) and Eccles Caravan
(#57, 1970)
16. red Golf, yellow caravan with flower
and stripe label ....$20 – 25
17. yellow Golf, yellow caravan with flower
and stripe label ....$20 – 25
18. green Golf, yellow caravan with flower
and stripe label ....$16 – 20
19. green Golf, beige caravan with flower
and stripe label ....$16 – 20
20. green Golf, beige caravan with
seagull label ....$20 – 25

Horse Box Transporter, Kenworth Conventional
Sleeper Cab, Convoy CY-6, 1982; HE-6, 1983
1. green cab, "BLUE GRASS FARMS" ...$10 – 12
2. green cab, tan trailer, no tampo ...$10 – 12
3. green cab, silver trailer,
"BLUE GRASS FARMS" ....$10 – 12
4. green cab, beige trailer, green and
orange stripes with horse silhouette ...$7 – 9

Indy 500 Closest Finish Ever, #32660, 1993
1. Two Formula Racers (#28, 1982; #16, 1984;
#74, 1996; #61, 1998; #246, 1994),
Valvoline, Mackenzie ....$8 – 10

Isuzu Amigo (#52, 1991) and Seafire (#5, 1975), TP-
129, 1992
1. red Isuzu, red Seafire with white hull and
"Surf Rider," white plastic trailer ......$9 – 12

Jaguar Matchmates, M-03, 1984
1. green Jaguar XK-120 (#22, 1984) and red Jaguar
SS-100 (#47, 1982) ....$14 – 18

Javelin and Pony Trailer, TP-3, 1976 (see **Pony Trailer Set**)

Jeep and Glider Trailer, TP-7, 1977 (see **Glider Set**)

Jeep Cherokee (#27, 1987) and Caravan (#31,
1977), TP-116, 1987
1. beige Jeep Cherokee with "Holiday Club,"
beige Caravan with "500" ....$9 – 12

Jeep Matchmates, M-03, 1984
1. brown Jeep (#5, 1982) and black Jeep (#20,
1982) ....$14 – 18

Kenworth Matchmates, M-06, 1984
1. black Kenworth Conventional Aerodyne
(#41, 1982) and metallic silver pearl Kenworth
COE Aerodyne (#45, 1982) ....$14 – 18
Lamborghini Miura, King Size K-24, 1969

1. metallic red ....$40 – 60
2. metallic bronze ....$14 – 18
3. metallic burgundy ....$14 – 18
4. metallic blue ....$14 – 18

Land Rover Ninety (#35, 1990) and Pony Trailer (#43,
1968), TP-130, 1992
1. white Land Rover, white Pony Trailer with
red roof, red and black stripes .....$9 – 12

Land Rover Ninety (#35, 1990) and Seafire Boat (#5,
1975), TP-121, 1989
1. white Land Rover with "County," white
Seafire with red hull, red design, white plastic
trailer with blue and red design ......$9 – 12
2. white Land Rover with "Bacardi," white
Seafire with white hull, "Bacardi," white
metal trailer (from #9 Boat and Trailer, 1966),
UK promotional ....$60 – 80

Locomotive (0-4-0 Steam Locomotive #43, 1978) and
Passenger Coach (#44, 1978), TP-124, 1991
1. green Locomotive with "British Railways,"
green Coach with "British Railways" ..$9 – 12

Long Haul Boat Transporter, TP-26, 1979
1. blue tractor with green windows, metallic
gray trailer with beige and red boat ..$40 – 50
2. blue tractor with amber windows, metallic
gray trailer with beige and red boat ..$14 – 18

Long Haul Box Container Truck, TP-24, 1979
1. red tractor, solid lettered
"Firestone" labels ....$30 – 40
2. red tractor, outlined lettered
"Firestone labels ....$40 – 50
3. red tractor, "Matchbox" labels ....$14 – 18
4. yellow tractor, "Matchbox" labels ..$40 – 50

Long Haul Covered Container Truck, TP-23, 1979
1. red tractor with amber windows, solid
lettered "Firestone" labels ....$14 – 18
2. red tractor with amber windows, outlined
lettered "Firestone" labels ....$14 – 18
3. red tractor with no windows, outlined
lettered "Firestone" labels ....$14 – 18

Long Haul Double Container Truck, TP-22, 1979
1. red tractor with amber windows, beige
containers with "OCL" labels ......$14 – 18
2. red tractor with amber windows, light blue
containers with "Sealand" labels ..$120 – 160
3. red tractor with amber windows, off-white
containers with "OCL" labels ....$14 – 18
4. red tractor with amber windows, red
containers with "NYK" labels .....$120 – 160

5. red tractor with amber windows, yellow containers with "OCL" labels . . . .$14 – 18
6. bronze tractor with amber windows, beige containers with "OCL" labels . . . .$14 – 18
7. bronze tractor with amber windows, cream containers with "OCL" labels . . . .$14 – 18
8. bronze tractor with amber windows, off – white containers with "OCL" labels . .$14 – 18
9. bronze tractor with no windows, beige containers with "OCL" labels . . . .$14 – 18
10. dark green tractor with amber windows, beige containers with "OCL" labels . .$120 – 160
11. dark green tractor with amber windows, orange containers with "OCL" labels . . . .$160 – 200

Long Haul Pipe Truck, TP-25, 1979
1. yellow tractor with amber windows, metallic gray flatbed with orange pipes . . . . .$40 – 50
2. yellow tractor with amber windows, black flatbed with orange pipes . . . .$40 – 50
3. dark green tractor with amber windows, metallic gray flatbed with orange pipes . . . .$14 – 18
4. dark green tractor with amber windows, black flatbed with orange pipes . . . .$14 – 18
5. bronze tractor with amber windows, black flatbed with orange pipes . . . .$80 – 100

Low Loader with Dodge Delivery Truck, Scania, Convoy CY-803, 1992, Europe
1. red . . . .$20 – 25

Mack Auxiliary Power Truck (#57, 1991-1997) and Chevrolet Ambulance (#41, 1978; #25, 1983), EM-83, 1992
1. fluorescent orange power truck, white ambulance, plastic accessories . . . . . .$7 – 9

Matra Rancho (#37, 1982), Inflatable Raft and Trailer, TP-110, 1984
1. navy blue Matra with design and white base, orange raft with white hull, no markings, black trailer, England cast . . . .$14 – 18
2. navy blue Matra with design and white base, orange raft with white hull, "SR," black trailer, England cast . . . .$14 – 18
3. navy blue Matra with design and white base, yellow raft with white hull, "SR," black trailer, England cast . . . .$16 – 20
4. black Matra with design and white base, orange raft with white hull, "SR," black trailer, England cast . . . .$14 – 18
5. orange Matra with design and black base, orange raft with white hull, "2," white trailer, England cast . . . .$14 – 18

Mercedes (see **Mercedes Benz**)

Mercedes Benz 280 GE G-Wagon (#30, 1984) and Dinghy, TP-131, 1992
1. white Mercedes Benz with orange roof and "Marine Rescue," fluorescent orange dinghy with gray hull and "Rescue," white trailer . . . .$9 – 12

Mercedes Benz 280 GE G-Wagon (#30, 1984) and Pony Trailer (#43, 1968), TP-117, 1987
1. white Mercedes Benz with "Polizei" and checkerboard design, white Pony Trailer with "Polizei" and checkerboard design . .$9 – 12
2. white Mercedes Benz with green "Polizei," green Pony Trailer with "Polizei" . . . . . .$9 – 12

Mercedes Benz 300 SE Staff Car (#46, 1968) and Mercedes Benz Ambulance (#3, 1968), TP-14, 1979
1. olive green Staff Car, olive green Ambulance . . . .$16 – 20

Mercedes Benz Ambulance and Mercury Fire Chief, TP-10, 1978 (see **Fire Chief and Ambulance**)

Mercedes Benz Ambulance and Staff Car, TP-14, 1979 (see **Mercedes Benz 300 SE Staff Car** and **Mercedes Benz Ambulance**)

Mercedes Benz C-111, King Size K-30, 1972
1. metallic gold, with battery compartment, Germany issue . . . .$135 – 160
2. metallic gold . . . .$15 – 20
3. lime green . . . .$14 – 18
4. blue . . . .$14 – 18
5. Bulgaria casting, various colors . . . . . .$35 – 60

Mercedes Benz Covered Truck (#1, 1968) and Trailer (#2, 1968), TP-1, 1976

1. **red with yellow canopies, "Transcontinental" labels** . . . .**$14 – 18**
2. powder blue with yellow canopies, "I.M.S." labels . . . .$24 – 32

Mercedes Benz G-Wagon and Dinghy, TP-131, 1992 (see **Mercedes Benz 280 GE G-Wagon and Dinghy**)

Mercedes Benz G-Wagon and Horse Box, TP-117, 1987 (see **Mercedes Benz 280 GE G-Wagon and Pony Trailer**)

Mercedes Benz G-Wagon and Inflatable Raft, TP-131, 1992 (see **Mercedes Benz 280 GE G-Wagon and Dinghy**)

Mercedes Benz Military Covered Truck (#1, 1968) **and Trailer** (#2, 1968), TP-15, 1977
1. army green truck, army green trailer with "48350USA" labels . . . .$150 – 180
2. army green truck with "48350USA" labels, army green trailer with "4TS702K" labels . .$150 – 180
3. olive green truck, olive green trailer with "48350USA" labels . . . .$16 – 20
4. olive green truck, olive green trailer with "4TS702K" labels . . . .$16 – 20

Mercedes Benz Staff Car and Ambulance, TP-14, 1979 (see **Mercedes Benz 300 SE Staff Car and Mercedes Benz Ambulance**)

Mercedes Benz Trac 1600 Turbo Farm Tractor (#73, 1990) **and Hay Trailer** (#40, 1967), TP-126, 1991
1. yellow and green tractor, yellow hay trailer . . . .$9 – 12

Mercedes Benz Unimog (#49, 1967) **and Trailer** (#2, 1968), TP-112, 1984
1. yellow with white canopies, "Alpine Rescue" . . . .$14 – 18
2. red with white canopies, "Unfall Rettung" . . . .$14 – 18
3. white with orange canopies, "GES" . .$14 – 18

Mercedes Benz Unimog (#49, 1967) **and Weasel** (#73, 1974), TP-13, 1979
1. olive green Unimog with "A" label, olive green Weasel . . . .$14 – 18

Mercury Fire Chief and Mercedes Benz Ambulance, TP-10, 1978 (see **Fire Chief and Ambulance**)

Mercury Police and Merryweather Fire Engine, TP-2, 1979 (see **Police Car and Fire Engine**)

Mercury Police and Blaze Buster Fire Engine, TP-2, 1980 (see **Police Car and Fire Engine**)

Military Alvis Stalwart (#61, 1966) **and Ford Heavy Wreck Truck** (#71, 1968), TP-16, 1979
1. olive green Alvis Stalwart with "3LGS64" labels, olive green wreck truck . . . . .$16 – 20

Military Ambulance and Staff Car (see **Mercedes Benz Staff Car and Ambulance**)

Military Dump Truck (Mack Dump Truck #28, 1968) and Case Bulldozer (#16, 1969), TP-16, 1977
1. army green dump truck, army green bulldozer . . . .$150 – 175
2. olive green dump truck, olive green bulldozer . . . .$16 – 20

Military Field Car (#18, 1969) **and Motorcycle** (Hondarora #18, 1975), TP-11, 1977
1. olive green Field Car with star label, oliver green Hondarora . . . .$30 – 50

Military Field Car (#18, 1969) **and Volkswagen Van** (#23, 1970), TP-12, 1977
1. olive green Field Car with "3RA391" label, olive green Volkswagen Van with "Ambulance" labels . . . .$16 – 20

Military Jeep (Jeep #38, 1976, or Jeep Hot Rod #2, 1971) **and Motorcycle** (Hondarora #18, 1975), TP-11, 1977
1. army green Jeep with star label, no gun, army green Hondarora . . . .$150 – 180
2. olive green Jeep with star label, no gun, olive green Hondarora . . . .$16 – 20
3. olive green Jeep with "21*11" label, no gun, olive green Hondarora . . . .$16 – 20
4. olive green Jeep with "21*11" label, gun, olive green Hondarora . . . .$16 – 20

Military Mercedes Benz Covered Truck and Trailer, TP-15, 1977 (see **Mercedes Benz Military Covered Truck** (#1, 1968) **and Trailer** (#2, 1968)

Military Scout (Stoat Armored Truck #28, 1974) **and Armored Car** (Weasel #73, 1974), TP-13, 1977
1. army green Stoat, army green Weasel . . . .$150 – 175
2. olive green Stoat, oliver green Weasel . .$14 – 18

Military Tanker (Freeway Gas Tanker #63, 1973) **and Radar Truck** (Badger Exploration Truck #16, 1974), TP-14, 1977
1. army green tanker with Canadian flag label, army green radar truck . . . .$160 – 180
2. army green tanker with French flag label, army green radar truck . . . .$150 – 175
3. olive green tanker with "High Octane" labels, olive green radar truck . . . .$16 – 20

Military Unimog and Weasel (see **Mercedes Benz Unimog and Weasel**)

Miura (see **Lamborghini Miura**)

Miura Seaburst Set, 10", King Size K-29, 1971 (K-24 Lamborghini Miura and K-25 Seaburst Power Boat) . . . .$25 – 40

Mod Tractor (#25, 1972) **and Hay Trailer** (#40, 1967) TP-2, 1976
    1.   red tractor, yellow hay trailer . . . . . .$16 – 20

Money Box Armored Car, King Size K-88, 1981
    1.   white, "Fort Knox" . . . .$12 – 16
    2.   white, "Matchbox" . . . .$12 – 16
    3.   white, "Volksbank Raiffeisenbank," Germany issue . . . .$40 – 50
    4.   red, "Caisse D'Epargne" . . . .$30 – 40

Motorcycle Set with three plastic motorcycles, TP-21, 1979 – Variations:
Renault 5TL (#21, 1978) and Motorcycle Trailer
    1.   blue Renault, blue trailer with yellow motorcycles . . . .$16 – 20
Datsun 260Z (#67, 1978) and Motorcycle Trailer
    2.   blue Datsun, blue trailer with yellow motorcycles . . . .$16 – 20
    3.   blue Datsun, blue trailer with lemon yellow motorcycles . . . .$16 – 20
Citroen SM (#51, 1972) and Motorcycle Trailer
    4.   blue Citroen, blue trailer, yellow motorcycles . . . .$9 – 12
    5.   blue Citroen, blue trailer, red motorcycles . . . .$30 – 40

NASA Tracking Vehicle, Peterbilt, Convoy CY-15, 1985
    1.   white with white trailer, "NASA" tampos . .$7 – 9

Nigel Mansell Twinpacks, NM-810, 1994
    1.   Formula 1 (#246, 1994) and Grand Prix Racer (#74, 1988; #14, 1989) . . . .$5 – 7
    2.   Formula 1 (#246, 1994) and Mission Chopper (#46, 1985 – 1997) . . . .$5 – 7
    3.   Formula 1 (#246, 1994) and Chevy Van (#68, 1979; #44, 1982; #26, 1991) . . . . . .$5 – 7

Peterbilt Quarry Truck (#30, 1982) and Atlas Excavator (#32, 1981), CS-82, 1992
    1.   yellow quarry truck with red dumper, yellow excavator with red bucket, plastic accessories . . . .$7 – 9

Petrol Tanker (also see **Gas Tanker, Mack AC Tanker, Tanker**)

Petrol Tanker, Kenworth C.O.E., Convoy CY-7, 1982; HE-7, 1983
    1.   white, "SUPERGAS" . . . .$10 – 12

Petrol Tanker, Peterbilt Conventional Aerodyne, Convoy CY-7, 1982; HE-7, 1983
    1.   black, "SUPERGAS" . . . .$10 – 12

Petrol Tanker, Scania, Convoy CY-17, 1985
    1.   white with white tank, "AMOCO" . . . . .$7 – 9
    2.   red with red tank, "TIZER" . . . .$12 – 15
    3.   white with white tank, "Diet 7-Up" . .$12 – 15
    4.   orange with red tank, "CADBURY'S FUDGE" . . . .$12 – 15
    5.   white with chrome tank, "SHELL" . . . . . .$7 – 9
    6.   white with white tank, "FEOSO" . . . .$40 – 45

Pipe Truck, TP-25, 1979 (see **Long Haul Pipe Truck**)

Pipe Truck, Mack, Convoy CY-31, 1992
    1.   red with yellow plastic pipes . . . .$6 – 9

Police Car and Fire Engine, TP-2, 1979 – Variations:
Mercury Police (#55, 1971) and Merryweather Fire Engine (#35, 1969), 1979
    1.   white police car, red fire engine . . . .$14 – 18
Mercury Police (#55, 1971) and Blaze Buster Fire Engine (#22, 1975), 1980
    2.   white police car, red fire engine . . . .$16 – 20

Pony Trailer Set, TP-3 – Variations:
AMX Javelin (#9, 1972) and Pony Trailer (#43, 1968)
    1.   red Javelin (doors cast shut), beige Pony Trailer . . . .$75 – 100
    2.   green Javelin (doors cast shut), beige Pony Trailer . . . .$14 – 18
    3.   green Javelin (doors cast shut), orange Pony Trailer . . . .$14 – 18
    4.   lime green Javelin (doors open), orange Pony Trailer . . . .$14 – 18
    5.   metallic blue Javelin (doors open), orange Pony Trailer . . . .$14 – 18
    6.   blue Javelin (doors cast shut), beige Pony Trailer . . . .$14 – 18
    7.   blue Javelin (doors cast shut) with white design, beige Pony Trailer . . . .$16 – 20
Jeep CJ6 (#53, 1977) and Pony Trailer (#43, 1968)
    8.   red Jeep, orange Pony Trailer . . . . . .$20 – 30
    9.   red Jeep, beige Pony Trailer . . . .$20 – 30
Field Car (#18, 1969) and Pony Trailer (#43, 1968)
    10. red Field Car with "44" label, beige Pony Trailer . . . .$30 – 40

Porsche 911 Turbo (#3, 1978) and Caravan (#31, 1977), TP-113, 1985
    1.   black Porsche with gold design, white Caravan with "Mobile 500" . . . .$16 – 20

Porsche 911 Turbo (#3, 1978) and Glider Trailer, TP-122, 1989

1. dark blue Porsche with yellow design, dark blue trailer with white glider and yellow design . . . .$9 – 12

2. yellow Porsche with spatter design, yellow trailer with spatter design and bright pink glider . . . .$9 – 12

Power Launch Transporter, DAF, Convoy CY-22, 1987

1. white, "LAKESIDE" with "SHARK" on boat . . . .$10 – 12
2. white, "P&G," "CG22" . . . .$10 – 12
3. white, "COAST GUARD" . . . .$7 – 9
4. white, "RESCUE 3" . . . .$4 – 5

Power Launch Transporter, Kenworth C.O.E., Convoy CY-14, 1985

1. white with white boat . . . .$10 – 12

Quarry Truck and Excavator, CS-82, 1992 (see **Peterbilt Quarry Truck and Atlas Excavator**)

Racing Car Transporter, Kenworth C.O.E., HE-10, 1983; Convoy CY-10, 1984

1. white with "TYRONE MALONE" and MB-66 Super Boss with green windows . . . . .$15 – 20
2. white with "TYRONE MALONE" and MB-66 Super Boss with red windows . . . .$20 – 25

Renault 5TL (#21, 1978) and Motorcycle Trailer, TP-106, 1984

1. white Renault with green design, yellow trailer with red motorcycles . . . .$14 – 18
2. white Renault with pink and yellow design, yellow trailer with red motorcycles . . . .$14 – 18
3. white Renault with pink and yellow design, yellow trailer with olive green motorcycles . . . .$16 – 20
4. white Renault with pink and yellow design, yellow trailer with black motorcycles . .$16 – 20
5. white Renault with pink and yellow design, silver pearl trailer with black motorcycles . .$16 – 20

Road Roller and Crane, CS-83, 1992 (see **Bomag Road Roller and Faun Mobile Crane**)

Rocket Transporter, Kenworth C.O.E., Convoy CY-2, 1982; HE-2, 1983

1. silver-gray cab, trailer with Skybusters SB-3 Space Shuttle . . . .$15 – 18
2. silver-gray cab, trailer with white plastic rocket . . . .$10 – 12
3. pearl silver cab, white rocket . . . .$7 – 9
4. white cab, white rocket . . . .$6 – 9
5. white cab, chrome rocket . . . .$4 – 5

Rocket Transporter, Kenworth T2000, Convoy CY-2, 1982; HE-2, 1999

1. black cab, black trailer, chrome trim, Germany . . . .$10 – 12

Shovel Transporter, Mack, Convoy CY-32, 1992

1. orange-yellow with MB-29 Shovel Nose Tractor . . . .$6 – 9

Shunter and Tipper, TP-20, 1979, TP-125, 1991 (see **Diesel Shunter and Side Tipper**)

Skip Truck, 4⁵⁄₁₆", King Size K-28, 1978

1. orange, "Hales" . . . .$14 – 18
2. red, "Hales" . . . .$14 – 18
3. blue and red, "Hoch & Tief," Germany issue . . . .$30 – 50

Snorkel (#63, 1982) and Foam Pumper (#54, 1984), EM-81, 1992

1. fluorescent orange snorkel, fluorescent orange pumper, plastic accessories . . .$7 – 9

Stretcha Fetcha and Fire Chief, TP-7, 1976 (see **Emergency Set**)

Superstar Transporter, Ford Aeromax, Convoy CY-109, 1991 – Two versions were issued as "Convoy/ Super Rigs" models. The rest are White Rose Collectibles variations.

1. red, "Melling Performance" . . . .$12 – 15
2. red, "Motorcraft" . . . .$12 – 15

White Rose Collectibles variations:

3. white, "Hooters Racing" . . . .$12 – 15
4. black, "Texaco Havoline," "Davey Allison" . . . .$12 – 15
5. white with dark blue container, "Goodyear Racing" . . . .$12 – 15
6. white with dark blue container, "Penn State Nittany Lions" . . . .$12 – 15
7. rust, "Washington Redskins Super Bowl Champions" . . . .$12 – 15
8. white, "Snickers Racing Team" . . . . .$12 – 15
9. black, "Stanley Mechanic Tools 92" . .$12 – 15
10. green with red container, "Merry Christmas White Rose Collectibles 1992" . . . .$200 – 250
11. gold, "Folger's" . . . .$20 – 25
12. blue with white container, "Bill Elliot 9" . . . .$20 – $25

Superstar Transporter, Ford Aeromax, Convoy CY-113, 1994 from White Rose Collectibles

1. metallic blue, "Family Channel" . . . .$12 – 15
2. blue, "Quality Care Racing" . . . .$12 – 15
3. white, "7 Exide Batteries" . . . .$12 – 15
4. white, "Hooters Racing" . . . .$12 – 15

5. black, "Fingerhut Racing" . . . .$12 – 15
6. white with blue container, "Colts 94" $10 – 12
7. white with light blue container,
   "Oilers 94" . . . .$10 – 12
8. white with dark blue container,
   "Chargers 94" . . . .$10 – 12
9. white with black container,
   "Raiders 94" . . . .$10 – 12
10. white with red container, "Bills 94" . .$10 – 12
11. yellow with red container,
   "Cardinals 94" . . . .$10 – 12
12. yellow with red container,
   "KC Chiefs 94" . . . .$10 – 12
13. yellow with green container,
   "Packers 94" . . . .$10 – 12
14. yellow with black container,
   "Steelers 94" . . . .$10 – 12
15. orange with red container,
   "Buccaneers 94" . . . .$10 – 12
16. orange with white container,
   "Browns 94" . . . .$10 – 12
17. orange with white container,
   "Bengals 94" . . . .$10 – 12
18. orange with turquoise container,
   "Dolphins 94" . . . .$10 – 12
19. red-brown with yellow container,
   "Redskins 94" . . . .$10 – 12
20. red with dark blue container,
   "Patriots 94" . . . .$10 – 12
21. red with black container, "Falcons 94" . .$10 – 12
22. silver and gray with dark blue container,
   "Cowboys 94" . . . .$10 – 12
23. gold with red container, "SF 49ers" . .$10 – 12
24. green and gold with black container,
   "Saints 94" . . . .$10 – 12
25. purple with yellow container,
   "Vikings" . . . .$10 – 12
26. dark blue with white container,
   "Giants 94" . . . .$10 – 12
27. dark blue with orange container,
   "Broncos 94" . . . .$10 – 12
28. bright blue with yellow container,
   "Broncos 94" . . . .$10 – 12
29. blue with yellow container, "Rams 94" . .$10 – 12
30. blue with gray container, "Lions 94" . .$10 – 12
31. green with gray container, "Eagles 94" . .$10 – 12
32. green with white container, "Jets 94" . .$10 – 12
33. bright green with gray container,
   "Seahawks 94" . . . .$10 – 12

Superstar Transporter, Kenworth, Convoy CY-104, 1989 – Matchbox issued this truck in three series, Superstar Transporters from White Rose Collectibles, "Days of Thunder" models based on the movie of the same name, and Indy 500 series models, resulting in over 50 total variations of this model.

Superstar Transporters from White Rose Collectibles:
1. white cab with "STP" logo, white container,
   "Richard Petty," "STP" . . . .$325 – 400
2. white, "Neil Bonnett," "CITGO" . . .$100 – 125
3. white, "Hardee's Racing" . . . .$100 – 125
4. black, silver-gray base, Macau cast, "Good
   wrench Racing Team . . . .$200 – 275
5. white with blue container,
   "Goodyear Racing" . . . .$75 – 100
6. white cab with red and blue tampos, white
   container, "Richard Petty," "STP" . .$100 – 125
7. black, black base, Thailand cast,
   "Goodwrench Racing Team" . . . .$100 – 125
8. gold cab, no "6" on doors, gold
   container, "Folger's" . . . .$60 – 75
9. gold cab with "6" on doors, gold
   container, "Folger's" . . . .$30 – 40
10. white, "Trop Artic," "Dick Trickle" . . . .$40 – 50
11. black, "Goodwrench Racing Team" and
   car pictured . . . .$25 – 30
12. dark blue, "94 Sunoco," no
   "Sterling Marlin" . . . .$400 – 425
13. dark blue, "94 Sunoco,"
   "Sterling Marlin" . . . .$375 – 400
14. white, "Crown Moroso" . . . .$60 – 75
15. black, "Texaco Havoline,"
   "Davey Allison" . . . .$24 – 32
16. white, "Richard Petty" with portrait . .$40 – 50
17. dark blue with white container, "Penn
   State 1855 – 1991" . . . .$12 – 15
18. white, "Trop Artic," "Lake Speed" . . .$25 – 30
19. blue, "Maxwell House Racing" . . . . .$12 – 15
20. white, "Ken Schraeder 25" . . . .$12 – 15
21. orange – yellow, "Kodak Racing" . . .$12 – 15
22. white, "Purolator" . . . .$20 – 25
23. white, "Western Auto 17" . . . .$16 – 20
24. white, "Country Time" . . . .$16 – 20
25. black, "MAC Tools" . . . .$30 – 35
26. black, "Mello Yello 42" . . . .$16 – 20
27. black, "Alliance" . . . .$20 – 25
28. yellow, "Pennzoil," "Waltrip" . . . . . .$12 – 15
29. white, "STP – Richard Petty Fan
   Appreciation Tour 1992" . . . .$20 – 25
30. white, "Baby Ruth Racing" . . . .$12 – 15
31. black, "Goodwrench Racing Team"
   with checkered flags . . . .$15 – 20
32. metallic blue, "Raybestos" . . . .$12 – 15
33. black, "Slim Jim Racing Team" . . . . .$12 – 15
34. white and green, "Quaker State" . . .$12 – 15
35. blue and white, "Evinrude 98" . . . . . .$12 – 15
36. white, "Jasper Engines 55" . . . .$12 – 15
37. black, "MAC Tools Racing,"
   "Harry Gant" . . . .$15 – 20
38. black, "Martin Birrane – Team Ireland" . .$12 – 15
39. white, "Penn State Nittany Lions – Happy
   Valley Express" . . . .$12 – 15

"Days of Thunder" versions:
    40. black, "Exxon 51" . . . .$30 – 40
    41. black and green, "Mello Yello 51" . .$30 – 40
    42. orange, "Hardees 18" . . . .$30 – 40
    43. pink with white container, "Superflo" . .$30 – 40
    44. white, "City Chevrolet" . . . .$30 – 40
Indy 500 versions:
    45. white and blue, "Valvoline" . . . .$10 – 12
    46. yellow, "Pennzoil 4" . . . .$10 – 12
    47. yellow, "Pennzoil 2" . . . .$10 – 12
    48. white, "Panasonic" . . . .$10 – 12
    49. white, "K-Mart," "Havoline" . . . . . .$12 – 15

Superstar Transporter, Kenworth, Convoy CY-110, 1992 from White Rose Collectibles
    1. black, "Rusty Wallace – Pontiac" . . .$12 – 15
    2. black, "TIC Racing 8" . . . .$12 – 15
    3. orange, "Pic-N-Pay Shoes" . . . .$12 – 15

Superstar Transporter, Kenworth T600, Convoy CY-112, 1994 from White Rose Collectibles
    1. red with green container, "Merry Christmas 1993" . . . .$175 – 225
    2. black with yellow container, "White Rose Series II in '94" . . . .$12 – 15
    3. yellow, "White House Apple Juice Racing" in pink lettering . . . .$12 – 15
    4. yellow, "White House Apple Juice Racing" in red lettering . . . .$20 – 25
    5. dark blue with yellow container, "Matchbox," "White Rose 29" . . . .$12 – 15
    6. black with red container, "Phillies – National League Champions 1993" . . . .$12 – 15
    7. white, "Factory Stores of America" . .$12 – 15
    8. yellow with red container, "Kelloggs Racing 5" . . . .$12 – 15
    9. white, "Manheim Auctions 7" . . . . . .$12 – 15
    10. black, "Shoe World 32" . . . .$12 – 15
    11. black, "Baltimore Orioles 94" . . . .$12 – 15
    12. black with red container, "65th All Star Game – Pittsburgh Pirates 1994" . . . .$12 – 15
    13. purple with black container, "Colorado Rockies" . . . .$12 – 15
    14. black, "Carolina Panthers – Inaugural Season 1995" . . . .$12 – 15

Toe Joe (#74, 1972) and Racing Mini (#29, 1970) (see **Breakdown Set**, TP-6, 1976)

Tractor and Hay Trailer, TP-11, 1979, TP-108, 1984 (see **Ford Tractor and Hay Trailer**)

Tractor and Hay Trailer, TP-126, 1991 (see **Mercedes Benz Trac 1600 Turbo Farm Tractor and Hay Trailer**)

Tractor and Trailer, TP-2, 1976 (see **Mod Tractor and Hay Trailer**)

Transport Set – The Londoner Bus (#17, 1972) and SRN6 Hovercraft (#72, 1972), TP-8, 1976
    1. red bus with "Swinging London" labels, white hovercraft . . . .$16 – 20

Unimog (see **Mercedes Benz Unimog**)

Volkswagen Golf (#7, 1976) and Pony Trailer (#43, 1968), TP-114, 1985
    1. black Golf with red design, beige Pony Trailer with silver shoes design . . . . . .$16 – 20

Volkswagen Golf GTi (#33, 1986; #56, 1986; #63, 1991) and Inflatable Raft, TP-120, 1989
    1. dark gray Volkswagen, orange raft with black hull, white trailer with red and blue design . . . .$9 – 12

Volkswagen Van and Field Car (see **Military Field Car and Volkswagen Van**)

Volvo Covered Truck and Trailer, TP-128, 1992 (see **Circus Set**)

Water Sporter, TP-18, 1979 – Variations:
AMX Javelin (#9, 1972) and Seafire (#5, 1975)
    1. red Javelin, dark red Seafire with white hull . . . .$60 – 80
Volkswagen Golf (#7, 1976) and Seafire (#5, 1975)
    2. red Golf, red Seafire with white hull . .$14 – 18
    3. red Golf, white Seafire with brown hull . . . .$120 – 160
    4. red Golf, white Seafire with blue hull . .$16 – 20

Weekender Set, TP-5, 1976 – Variations:
Ford Capri (#54, 1971), Boat and Trailer (#9, 1966), 1980
    1. orange Capri, blue and white Boat and Trailer . . . .$16 – 20
Hot Rocker (#67, 1973), Boat and Trailer (#9, 1966)
    2. red-orange Hot Rocker, blue and white Boat and Trailer . . . .$16 – 20
Ford Escort RS2000 (#9, 1978), Boat and Trailer (#9, 1966)
    3. white Escort with "Dunlop" labels, blue and white Boat and Trailer . . . .$40 – 60
    4. white Escort with "Phantom" labels, blue and white Boat and Trailer . . . .$40 – 60
    5. blue Escort with "Phantom" labels, blue and white Boat and Trailer . . . .$40 – 60
Lotus Europa (#5, 1969), Boat and Trailer (#9, 1966)
    6. black Europa with "JPS," blue and white Boat and Trailer . . . .$40 – 60

Porsche 911 Turbo (#3, 1978), Boat and Trailer (#9, 1966)
7. brown Porsche, blue and white
Boat and Trailer . . . .$40 – 60
Volkswagen Golf (#7, 1976), Boat and Trailer (#9, 1966)
8. red Golf, blue and white
Boat and Trailer . . . .$14 – 18

Wrecker and Car (see **Breakdown Set**)

Zoo Truck and Eccles Caravan, TP-124, 1989 . .$18 – 24

Matchbox Buildings

Auto Park, AP-1, 1971 . . . .$140 – 180

Compact Garage, MG-7, 1984 . . . .$24 – 32

Deluxe Garage, MG-6, 1984 . . . .$24 – 32

Emergency Station, 580101, 1974 . . . .$60 – 80

Gearshift Garage, MG-9, 1987 . . . .$24 – 32
Matchbox Fire Station, MF-1, 1963
1. ivory with green roof, brick front . . .$180 – 220
2. white with red roof, brick front . . . . . .$80 – 110
3. white with red roof, smooth front . .$120 – 160

Matchbox One Story Garage, MG-1, 1959
1. yellow . . . .$180 – 240
2. red . . . .$180 – 240

Matchbox Service Station, MG-1, 1968 . . . .$80 – 110

Matchbox Two Story Garage, MG-1, 1961
1. "Esso," yellow with red base . . . .$180 – 240
2. "BP," white with green base . . . .$120 – 160

Service Station, MG-2, 1979 . . . .$60 – 80

Super Garage, MG-4, 1981 . . . .$50 – 70

Texaco Garage, MG-3, 1979 . . . .$60 – 80

Part 3: Other Matchbox Vehicles – Sea Kings, Skybusters, Star Cars

SEA KINGS

In 1976 a line of military ship models was introduced and named Sea Kings. The series, however, was short lived and only produced 10 models.

Aircraft Carrier, 8¾", SK-304, 1976 . . . .$12 – 15	Frigate, 8⅝", SK-301, 1976 . . . .$12 – 15
Anti-Aircraft Cruiser, 8⅛", SK-310, 1977 . . . . .$12 – 15	Guided Missile Destroyer, 8¹⁵⁄₁₆", SK-308, 1976 . .$12 – 15
Battleship, 8½", SK-303, 1976 . . . .$12 – 15	Helicopter Carrier, 8¼", SK-307, 1976 . . . .$12 – 15
Convoy Escort, 7⅞", SK-306, 1976 . . . .$12 – 15	Submarine, 8⅛", SK-309, 1977 . . . .$12 – 15
Corvette, 7⅞", SK-302, 1976 . . . .$12 – 15	Submarine Chaser, 7⅞", SK-305, 1976 . . . . . .$12 – 15

SKYBUSTERS, AIRPORT/AIRFORCE

These small-scale aircraft, typically about 3½ inches long, were introduced in 1973. Around 1995, Skybusters were issued as Airport or Airforce models, depending on whether the model represented a military or commercial aircraft. Current models are available in blister packs for around $4 each and are divided into two groups for marketing purposes as either Commercial or Military models.

A300 Airbus, SB-28, 1981
1. white and silver-gray, "Lufthansa" . . . .$6 – 8
2. white, "Alitalia" . . . .$6 – 8
3. white, "Air France" . . . .$6 – 8
4. light blue and silver-gray, "Korean Air" . .$6 – 8

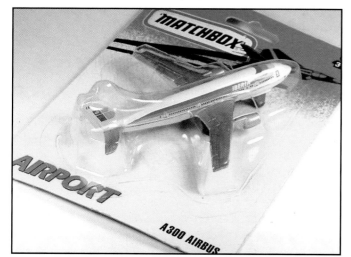

5. **white, "Iberia"** . . . .$6 – 8
6. white, "Air Inter" . . . .$60 – 75
7. white and silver-gray, "Swissair" . . . .$6 – 8
8. white, "Air Malta" . . . .$15 – 18

A300B Airbus, SB-3, 1973
1. white and gray, "Air France" . . . .$8 – 10
2. white and gray, "Lufthansa" . . . .$6 – 8

Alpha Jet, SB-11, 1973
1. metallic red and white . . . .$8 – 10
2. blue and red . . . .$10 – 12
3. blue . . . .$8 – 10
4. white and red . . . .$8 – 10

B.AE 146, SB-38, 1992
1. white, "Dan – Air" . . . .$4 – 5

2. **white, "Thai"** . . . .$6 – 8

Bell Jet Ranger Helicopter, SB-33, 1990
1. white and blue, "Sky Ranger" . . . .$4 – 5

Boeing 737-300, SB-40, 1992
1. white and dark blue, "Brittania" . . . . . .$4 – 5

2. **light blue and silver-gray, "KLM"** . . . . .$4 – 5

Boeing 747, SB-10, 1973
1. white and dark blue, "BOAC" . . . .$8 – 10
2. white and dark blue, "British Airways" . .$8 – 10
3. white and dark blue, "Qantas" . . . . . .$8 – 10
4. white and silver-gray, "United
   States of America" . . . .$12 – 15
5. white and silver-gray, "MEA" . . . .$12 – 15
6. white and silver plated, "BOAC," on
   ashtray/stand . . . .$40 – 50
7. white and gold plated, "British Airways,"
   on ashtray/stand . . . .$40 – 50
8. white with silver wings, "El Al" . . . .$8 – 10
9. white and dark blue, "British . . . .$12 – 15
10. white and silver-gray, "Cathay Pacific" . .$6 – 8
11. white and silver-gray,
    "British Caledonia" . . . .$8 – 10
12. white and silver-gray, "Lufthansa" . . . .$6 – 8
13. white and silver-gray, "Pan Am" . . . .$12 – 15
14. white, "Virgin" . . . .$6 – 8

15. light blue and silver-gray, "KLM" . . . . . .$6 – 8
16. white and silver-gray, "Air Nippon" . .$12 – 15
17. lime and white, "Aer Lingus" . . . .$6 – 8
18. white, "South African Airways" . . . . .$12 – 15
19. white and silver-gray, "Saudi" . . . .$4 – 5
20. white and silver-gray, "Olympic" . . . . .$4 – 5

Boeing 747-400, SB-31, 1990

1. light gray and dark blue, "British Airways" . . .$5 – 6
2. white and silver-gray, "Cathay Pacific" . .$4 – 5
3. white and silver-gray, "Lufthansa" . . . .$4 – 5
4. white and silver-gray,
   "Signapore Airlines" . . . .$4 – 5

Boeing Stearman Biplane, SB-39, 1992
1. orange-yellow, "Crunchie," printing
   on underside of wings . . . .$25 – 30
2. orange-yellow, "Crunchie," no printing
   on underside of wings . . . .$4 – 5
3. white, "Circus Circus" . . . .$4 – 5

Cessna 210, SB-14, 1973
1. orange-yellow and white . . . .$8 – 10

Cessna 210 Float Plane, SB-26, 1981
1. red and white . . . .$6 – 8
2. black and white . . . .$6 – 8
3. red, "Fire" . . . .$4 – 5
4. white, "007 James Bond" . . . .$8 – 10

Cessna 402, SB-9, 1973
1. light green and white . . . .$8 – 10
2. dark green and white . . . .$5 – 7
3. brown and beige . . . .$6 – 8
4. white and red,
   "DHL World-Wide Express" . . . .$5 – 6
5. blue and yellow . . . .$4 – 6

Corsair A7D, SB-2, 1973
1. dark green and white . . . .$8 – 10
2. khaki and white with brown and
   green camouflage . . . .$6 – 8
3. orange and white . . . .$5 – 6

Corsair F4U, SB-16, 1975
1. metallic blue . . . .$6 – 8
2. orange . . . .$6 – 8

Douglas DC-10, SB-13, 1973
1. white and red, "Swissair" . . . .$8 – 10
2. white and silver-gray, "Swissair" . . . . . .$8 – 10
3. whiteand silver-gray, "United" . . . .$8 – 10
4. white and silver-gray, "Lufthansa" . . . .$6 – 8
5. white and silver-gray, "Alitalia" . . . . . .$6 – 8
6. white, "Thai," Macau cast . . . .$6 – 8
7. white, "Thai," Thailand cast . . . .$4 – 5
8. silver and red, "Aeromexico" . . . .$6 – 8
9. silver-gray, "American" . . . .$6 – 8
10. white, "UTA" . . . .$60 – 75
11. white, "Scandinavian" . . . .$4 – 5
12. white and silver-gray, "Sabena" . . . . . .$4 – 5

Douglas Skyhawk, SB-12, 1973
1. dark blue and white, "Navy" . . . .$8 – 10
2. dark blue and white, "Marines" . . . . .$8 – 10

F-16, SB-24, 1979
1. white and red, "USAF," no side labels . .$6 – 8
2. white and red, "USAF," "United States
   Air Force" on sides . . . .$5 – 6

3. white with no markings, Graffic Traffic . .$6 – 8

Fairchild A10 Thunderbolt (dubbed "Warthog" during Desert Storm, Persian Gulf War), SB-32, 1990
1. dark gray with green camouflage . . . .$4 – 5

Grumman F-14 Tomcat, SB-30, 1989

1. **gray and white, "Navy"** . . . .$4 – 5

Harrier Jet, SB-27, 1981
1. white and red . . . .$6 – 8
2. light gray and white . . . .$5 – 6
3. dark blue and white, "Royal Navy" . . .$5 – 6
4. light green and white, "Marines" . . . . .$5 – 6

Hawk, SB-37, 1992
1. red, "Royal Air Force" . . . .$5 – 7

Helicopter, SB-20, 1977

1. **olive, "Army"** . . . .$8 – 10
2. white and light blue, "Coast Guard" . .$6 – 8
3. white and red, "Police" . . . .$6 – 8
4. dark blue and white, "Air-Aid" . . . .$6 – 8
5. dark blue, "Gendarmerie JAB" . . . . .$60 – 75

Helicopter (also see **Rescue Helicopter**)

Junkers 87B, SB-7, 1973
1. green with swastikas . . . .$8 – 10
2. black with swastikas . . . .$80 – 90
3. black with beige and brown . . . .$8 – 10

Learjet, SB-1, 1973
1. yellow and white, "D-IDLE" . . . .$8 – 10
2. red, "Datapost" . . . .$6 – 8
3. purple and white, "Federal Express" . . .$5 – 7
4. white, "G – JCB" . . . .$6 – 8
5. white, "U. S. Air Force" . . . .$4 – 5
6. purple, "U. S. Air Force" . . . .$5 – 6
7. white and orange, "Q-Xpress Freight Delivery Service" . . . .$4 – 6
8. white, "DHL" . . . .$4 – 5

Lightning SB-21 1977
1. olive . . . .$8 – 10
2. silver-gray . . . .$8 – 10

Lockheed A130 (see **Lockheed C-130 Hercules**)

Lockheed C-130 Hercules, SB-34, 1990

1. **white, "USCG"** . . . .$4 – 5

Lockheed F-117A Stealth, SB-26, 1990; SB-36, 1991

1. **dark gray, "USAF"** . . . .$4 – 5
2. white, no markings, Graffic Traffic . . . . .$5 – 6

Lockheed SR-71 Blackbird, SB-29, 1989
1. black, "U. S. Air Force" . . . .$4 – 5

MIG 21, SB-6, 1973
1. blue and white . . . .$8 – 10
2. silver-gray . . . .$5 – 6
3. black . . . .$5 – 6
4. light purple . . . .$5 – 6
5. silver . . . .$4 – 5

MiL M24 Hind-D Chopper, SB-35, 1990

1. brown and gray . . . .**$4 – 5**
2. camouflage khaki and army green . . .$4 – 5

Military Helicopter, Skybusters 2003
1. avocado green and bright purple . . . . .**$4 – 5**

Mirage F1, SB-4, 1973
1. red with bullseye on wings . . . .$8 – 10

2. orange and brown, "122-18" . . . .$5 – 6
3. yellow . . . .$4 – 5
4. white, "ZE-164" . . . .$4 – 5
5. pink . . . .$5 – 6
6. blue . . . .$4 – 5

Mission Chopper, SB-12, 1992 variation of #46, 1985 – 1997
1. army green with tan base and skids, tan tail and blades, star and emblem . . . .$2 – 3

NASA Space Shuttle, SB-3, 1980
1. white and gray . . . .$5 – 6

Phantom F4E SB-15 1975
1. metallic red and white . . . .$6 – 8
2. cherry red and white . . . .$6 – 8
3. gray, "Marines," Macau cast . . . .$5 – 6
4. gray, "Marines," Thailand cast . . . .$3 – 4
5. pink, "Marines" . . . .$5 – 6

Piper Comanche, SB-19, 1977
1. red and yellow . . . .$6 – 8
2. white, "XP" . . . .$6 – 8
3. beige and dark blue, "Comanche," Macau cast . . . .$5 – 6
4. beige and dark blue, "Comanche," Thailand cast . . . .$4 – 5

Pitts Special Biplane, SB-12, 1980
1. metallic red and white . . . .$6 – 8
2. dark green and white . . . .$8 – 10
3. blue and white . . . .$8 – 10
4. red, "Fly Virgin Atlantic" . . . .$4 – 5
5. white, no markings, Graffic Traffic . . . .$6 – 8
6 white, "Circus Circus" . . . .$6 – 8

Ram Rod, SB-17, 1976
1. red . . . .$8 – 10

Rescue Helicopter, SB-25, 1979
1. yellow . . . .$6 – 8
2. white . . . .$8 – 10
3. dark blue, "Royal Air Force Rescue" . . .$6 – 8
4. white, "Shell" . . . .$6 – 8
5. white and red, "007" . . . .$8 – 10

Space Shuttle (see **NASA Space Shuttle**)

Spitfire, SB-8, 1973
1. dark brown and gold . . . .$12 – 15
2. metallic green and gold . . . .$8 – 10
3. gold plated on pen stand . . . .$40 – 50
4. light brown and khaki . . . .$8 – 10
5. khaki with green camouflage . . . . . .$20 – 25

SST Super Sonic Transport, SB-23, 1979
1. white, "Air France" ....$5 – 7
2. white, "Singapore" ....$15 – 20
3. white, "Supersonic Airlines" ....$4 – 5
4. white, "Singapore Airlines" ....$75 – 100

5. **white, "British Airways"** ....$4 – 5
6. white, "Heinz 57" ....$20 – 25
7. white with no markings, Graffic Traffic ..$5 – 6

Starfighter F104, SB-5, 1973
1. white with maple leaf labels ....$8 – 10
2. red with maple leaf labels ....$8 – 10

Tornado, SB-22, 1978

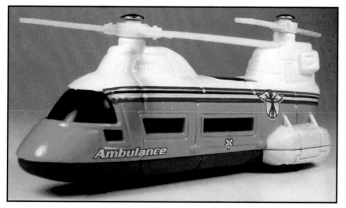

1. **light gray and white** ....$6 – 8
2. dark gray and white ....$6 – 8
3. red and white ....$6 – 8
4. light purple and white ....$4 – 5

Transport Helicopter, Skybusters 2003

1. **turquoise and white** ....$4 – 5

2. orange, white and red ....$4 – 5

Wild Wind, SB-18, 1976
1. lime green and white ....$8 – 10

CHARACTER TOYS

Disney Characters

Donald Duck's Beach Buggy, WD-2, 1979
1. Hong Kong cast ....$20 – 30
2. Macau cast ....$60 – 80

Donald Duck's Ice Cream Van, WD-11, 1979
1. Hong Kong cast ....$30 – 40
2. Macau cast ....$60 – 80

Donald Duck's Jeep, WD-6, 1979

1. Hong Kong cast ....$20 – 30

2. Macau cast . . . .$60 – 80

Goofy's Beetle, WD-3, 1979
1. Hong Kong cast . . . .$20 – 30
2. Macau cast . . . .$60 – 80

Goofy's Sports Car, WD-9, 1979
1. Hong Kong cast . . . .$30 – 40
2. Macau cast . . . .$60 – 80

Goofy's Train, WD-10, 1980
1. Hong Kong cast . . . .$60 – 80
2. Macau cast . . . .$70 – 90

Jiminy Cricket's Old Timer, WD-8, 1979
1. Hong Kong cast . . . .$20 – 30
2. Macau cast . . . .$60 – 80

Mickey Mouse's Corvette, WD-12, 1980
1. Hong Kong cast . . . .$30 – 40
2. Macau cast . . . .$60 – 80

Mickey Mouse's Fire Engine, WD-1, 1979
1. Hong Kong cast . . . .$30 – 40
2. Macau cast . . . .$60 – 80

Mickey Mouse's Jeep, WD-5, 1979

1. Hong Kong cast . . . .**$20 – 30**
2. Macau cast . . . .$60 – 80

Minnie Mouse's Lincoln, WD-4, 1979

1. Hong Kong cast . . . .**$20 – 30**
2. Macau cast . . . .$60 – 80

Pinocchio's Traveling Theater, WD-7, 1979

1. Hong Kong cast . . . .**$30 – 40**
2. Macau cast . . . .$60 – 80

Looney Tunes

Bugs Bunny Group C Racer, 1994 . . . . $4 – 5

Daffy Duck 4x4 Pickup, 1994 . . . . $4 – 5

Road Runner Dragster, 1994 . . . . $4 – 5

Bugs Bunny Lumina, 1994 . . . . $4 – 5

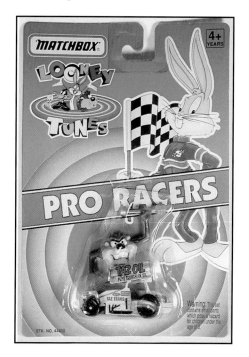

Tasmanian Devil's Sprint Racer, 1994 . . . .$4 – 5

Wile E. Coyote Lumina, 1994 . . . .$4 – 5

Popeye

Bluto's Road Roller, CS-14, 1981 . . . .$40 – 50

Olive Oyl's Sports Car, CS-15, 1981 . . . .$40 – 50

Popeye's Spinach Wagon, CS-13, 1981 . . . . .$40 – 50

Sesame Street

Baby Bear's Buggy, 1998 . . . .$4 – 5

Bert's Tow Truck, 1997 . . . .$4 – 5

Big Bird's Dune Buggy, 1998 . . . .$4 – 5

Big Bird's Fire Engine, 1997 . . . .$4 – 5

Big Bird's Mail Van, 1998 . . . .$4 – 5

Cookie Monster's Airplane, 1998 . . . .$4 – 5

Cookie Monster's School Bus, 1997 . . . .$4 – 5

Elmo's Cement Truck, 1998 . . . .$4 – 5

Elmo's Taxi, 1997 . . . .$4 – 5

Elmo's Train, 1999 . . . .$4 – 5

Elmo's Watercraft, 1999 . . . .$4 – 5

Ernie's Car Carrier, three-piece set, 1999 . . .$12 – 16

Ernie's Cement Mixer, 1998 . . . .$4 – 5

Ernie's Dump Truck, 1997 . . . .$4 – 5

Ernie's Police Car, 1997 . . . .$4 – 5

Oscar's Garbage Truck, 1997 . . . .$4 – 5

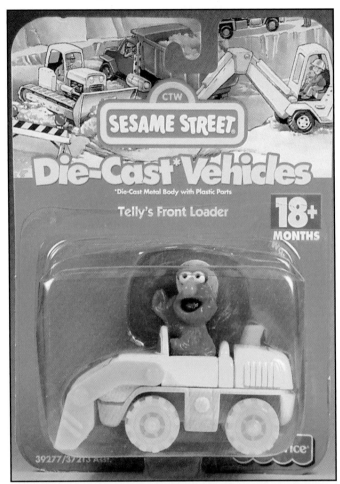

Telly's Front Loader, 1998 . . . . **$4 – 5**

The Count's Sports Car, 1999 . . . .$4 – 5

Zoe's Sports Car, 1997 . . . .$4 – 5

Star Cars Collection

Star Cars Series I, 1998:
#1 "Grease," '33 Willys . . . .$4 – 6
#2 "Taxi" Sunshine Cab Ford LTD . . . .$4 – 6
#3 "Brady Bunch" Mercury Sable Station Wagon . .$4 – 6
#4 "Happy Days" '56 Ford Pick-Up . . . .$4 – 6
#5 "MASH" 4077 Jeep CJ . . . .$4 – 6
#6 "Mission: Impossible" Surveillance Van . . . .$4 – 6

Star Cars Series 2, 1998:
#7 "Magnum P.I." Ferrari 308 GTS . . . .$4 – 6
#8 "Miami Vice" Ferrari Testarossa Convertible . .$4 – 6
#9 "Jaws" Amity Police Launch with Shark . . .$4 – 6
#10 "Animal House" '62 Corvette . . . .$4 – 6
#11 "Adam-12" Police Car . . . .$4 – 6
#12 "Smokey & The Bandit" Pontiac
     Trans Am T-Roof . . . .$4 – 6

Star Cars Series 3, 1999:
#13 "Mork & Mindy" Jeep CJ . . . .$4 – 6
#14 "Laverne & Shirley" Shotz Brewery FJ
     Holden Panel Van . . . .$4 – 6
#15 "Knight Rider" Trans Am . . . .$4 – 6
#16 "The Untouchables" Ford Model T . . . .$4 – 6
#17 "American Graffiti" Hot Rod . . . .$4 – 6
#18 "Top Gun" Fighter Jet . . . .$4 – 6

Star Cars Character Cars:
Ace Ventura, Ford LTD Police Car, #96114 . . .$10 – 14
Animal House, 1962 Chevrolet Corvette,
     #96112, 2000 . . . .$9 – 12
Fonzie, Harley-Davidson Motorcycle,
     #98111, 2000 . . . .$8 – 10
Frankenstein, Ford Model T Van, #96107, 2000 . .$9 – 12
Freddy Kreuger, Chevrolet Van, #38247, 2000 . .$8 – 10
Gilligan, "S. S. Minnow" Police Launch,
     #96110, 2000 . . . .$8 – 10
I Dream of Jeannie, '69 Camaro, #96106, 2000 . .$8 – 10
Jason, Jeep Cherokee, #38248, 1999 . . . . . .$8 – 10
Leatherface, '56 Ford Pickup, #92082, 2001 . .$10 – 14
Rocky, Pontiac Trans Am T-Roof, #96113, 2000 . .$9 – 12
The Mask, Ford LTD Police Car, #96109, 2000 . .$8 – 10
Wolfman, Ford Model A Van, #96108, 2000 . . .$9 – 12

Thunderbirds

A new Thunderbirds live-action movie released in theaters in 2004 recalls the animated adventures of the Tracy family and its secret high-tech "International Rescue" organization. The original 1960s children's television series was produced by Gerry Anderson, applying his trademark "Supermarionation" — animation using marionette puppets, high drama, and spectacular special effects. Matchbox produced a series of "Thunderbirds" vehicles in 1992 to celebrate the TV show's re-release in Great Britain.

Thunderbirds vehicles and sets:
International Rescue Set . . . .$40 – 60
Lady Penelope's Fab 1, TB-005, 1992 . . . .$12 – 16
The Mole, #41785 . . . .$12 – 16

Thunderbird 1, TB-001, 1992 . . . .**$9 – 12**
Thunderbird 2 and 4, TB-002, 1992 . . . .$18 – 24
Thunderbird 3, TB-003, 1992 . . . .$9 – 12
Thunderbirds Gift Set by Vivid Imaginations
    of Canada, 1991 . . . .$75 – 100
Thunderbirds Anniversary Set, 1996,
    gold plated . . . .$120 – 160
Tracy Island playset, #41720 . . . .$9 – 12

Thunderbirds action figures, 1994:
Alan Tracy . . . .$35 – 45
Gordon Tracy . . . .$35 – 45
Scott Tracy . . . .$35 – 40
Virgil Tracy . . . .$35 – 45

Stingray

    After the success of the "Thunderbirds" vehicles and sets, Matchbox issued a series of "Stingray" vehicles and action figures from another of Gerry Anderson's 1960s television action adventure shows.

Stingray Vehicles and Playsets:
Marineville Playset . . . .$60 – 80
Stingray Action Playset . . . .$40 – 50
Stingray and Terrorfish, #43200 . . . .$12 – 16

Stingray Action Figures:
Commander Shore . . . .$8 – 10
Marina . . . .$8 – 10
Phones . . . .$8 – 10
Titan . . . .$8 – 10
Troy Tempest . . . .$8 – 10

Part 4: Matchbox Dolls and Action Figures, Toys and Games

ABBA - introduced in 1978
Anna, AB-101 . . . .$90 – 120
Bennie, AB-103 . . . .$90 – 120
Bjorn, AB-104 . . . .$90 – 120
Frida, AB-102 . . . .$90 – 120

DISCO GIRLS - Vogue dolls, introduced in 1974
Britt, DG-101 . . . .$40 – 50
Dee, DG-100 . . . .$40 – 50
Disco Bride, DG-150 . . . .$40 – 50
Disco Darling, DG-153 . . . .$40 – 50
Disco Date, DG-151 . . . .$40 – 50
Disco Deb, DG-152 . . . .$40 – 50
Domino, DG-102 . . . .$40 – 50
Tia, DG-103 . . . .$40 – 50
Tony, DG-104 . . . .$40 – 50

FIGHTING FURIES - action figures, introduced in 1974
Black McCoy, FF-103 . . . .$50 – 60
Captain Peg Leg, FF-100 . . . .$50 – 60
Crazy Horse, FF-104, FF-106 . . . .$50 – 60
Ghost of Captain Kidd, FF-102 . . . .$50 – 60
Hook, FF-101 . . . .$50 – 60
Kid Cortez, FF-105 . . . .$50 – 60

MISS MATCHBOX - character dolls, introduced in 1974
Alice in Wonderland, M01 . . . .$16 – 20
Blue Belle, M11 . . . .$16 – 20
Calamity Jane, M04 . . . .$16 – 20
Cookie Kate, M09 . . . .$16 – 20
Cosy Cathy, M07 . . . .$16 – 20
Jilly Jodhpur, M08 . . . .$16 – 20
Mod Millie, M14 . . . .$16 – 20
Party Patti, M13 . . . .$16 – 20
Penny Playmate, M16 . . . .$16 – 20
Polly Painter, M05 . . . .$16 – 20
Sailor Sue, M02 . . . .$16 – 20
Sally Stewardess, M15 . . . .$16 – 20

PEE WEE'S PLAYHOUSE

    Of special note is a popular line of toys spawned from the TV series *Pee Wee's Playhouse*, a popular but controversial cutting-edge show for kids hosted by Paul Ruben as Pee Wee Herman. The show only lasted for two years, from 1989 to 1990, but generated a lot of fans as well as detractors. Values on the various characters from the show are rising steadily since the show's demise and Ruben's notorious incident in an adult movie theater.

Pee Wee's Playhouse Characters

Billy Baloney, 1989 . . . .$40 – 55
Chairry, small, 1989 . . . .$12 – 16
Chairry, large, 1989 . . . .$40 – 55
Conkey, 1989 . . . .$16 – 20
Cowboy Curtis, 1989 . . . .$12 – 16
Globey & Randi, 1989 . . . .$16 – 20
Jambi & The Puppet Band, 1989 . . . .$16 – 20
King of Cartoons, 1989 . . . .$16 – 20
Magic Screen, 1989 . . . .$12 – 16
Miss Yvonne, 1989 . . . .$12 – 16
Pee Wee Herman, articulated arms
    and legs, 5¾" tall, 1989 . . . .$12 – 16
Pee Wee Herman and Scooter, 1989 . . . . . .$30 – 40
Pee Wee Herman doll, non-talking, 1989 . . .$40 – 55
Pee Wee Herman doll, talking, 1989 . . . . . .$40 – 55
Pee Wee Herman's Ventriloquist Dummy, 1990 . .$90 – 120
Pee Wee's Playhouse Playset, #3550, 1989 . .$90 – 120
Pee Wee's Scooter riding toy, 1989 . . . . . .$275 – 325
Pterri, small, 1989 . . . .$16 – 20
Pterri, large, 1989 . . . .$40 – 55
Reba, 1990 . . . .$18 – 24
Ricardo, 1990 . . . .$16 – 20
Vance the Talking Pig, 1990 . . . .$40 – 55

POOCH TROOP – plush toys, introduced in 1989
Colonel Ollie Collie . . . .$24 – 32
Doc Bernard . . . .$24 – 32
Sergeant Barker . . . .$24 – 32
Top Dog . . . .$24 – 32

POPSICLE KIDS – introduced in 1990
Berry Blue . . . .$12 – 16
Grape Cakes . . . .$12 – 16
La De Lime . . . .$12 – 16

Lotta Lime . . . .$12 – 16
Merry Cherry . . . .$12 – 16
Ooh La Orange . . . .$12 – 16

REAL MODELS – introduced in 1990
Beverly Johnson . . . .$20 – 30
Cheryl Tiegs . . . .$20 – 30
Christie Brinkley . . . .$20 – 30

RUBIK'S
Rubik's Clock, 1989 . . . .$18 – 22
Rubik's Cube, 1989 . . . .$9 – 12
Rubik's Dice, 1990 . . . .$18 – 22
Rubik's Fifteen, 1990 . . . .$18 – 22
Rubik's Illusion Game, 1989 . . . .$18 – 22
Rubik's Link The Rings, 1987 . . . .$12 – 16
Rubik's Magic Picture Games, 1988
    1. Crazy Orchestra . . . .$7 – 9
    2. Dinosaur Days . . . .$7 – 9
    3. Monster Sports . . . .$7 – 9
    4. Octopus's Garden . . . .$7 – 9
Rubik's Magic Puzzle, 1987 . . . .$12 – 16
Rubik's Magic Strategy Game, 1987 . . . .$20 – 30
Rubik's Tangle, 1990 . . . .$18 – 22
Rubik's Triamid, 1990 . . . .$18 – 22

SUKY, SUSY, PATTY DOLLS – introduced in 1976
Ballerina, S01 . . . .$12 – 16
Bedtime, S07 . . . .$12 – 16
Horse Rider, S04 . . . .$12 – 16
Nurse, S02 . . . .$12 – 16
Shopper, S06 . . . .$12 – 16
Skater, S05 . . . .$12 – 16
Swimmer, S08 . . . .$12 – 16
Tennis Pro, S03 . . . .$12 – 16

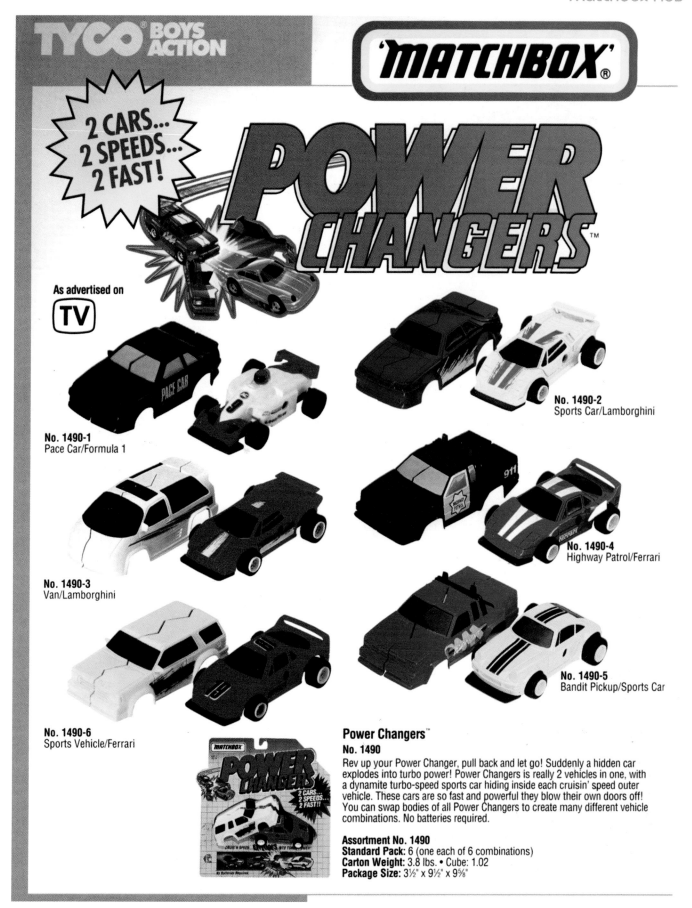

TYCO® BOYS ACTION

'MATCHBOX'®

2 CARS...
2 SPEEDS...
2 FAST!

POWER CHANGERS™

As advertised on **TV**

No. 1490-1
Pace Car/Formula 1

No. 1490-2
Sports Car/Lamborghini

No. 1490-3
Van/Lamborghini

No. 1490-4
Highway Patrol/Ferrari

No. 1490-5
Bandit Pickup/Sports Car

No. 1490-6
Sports Vehicle/Ferrari

Power Changers™
No. 1490

Rev up your Power Changer, pull back and let go! Suddenly a hidden car explodes into turbo power! Power Changers is really 2 vehicles in one, with a dynamite turbo-speed sports car hiding inside each cruisin' speed outer vehicle. These cars are so fast and powerful they blow their own doors off! You can swap bodies of all Power Changers to create many different vehicle combinations. No batteries required.

Assortment No. 1490
Standard Pack: 6 (one each of 6 combinations)
Carton Weight: 3.8 lbs. • **Cube:** 1.02
Package Size: 3½" x 9½" x 9⅝"

Tyco Toys, 1993, pg. 26

Harley-Davidson® LIMITED EDITION COLLECTOR SET

No. 76272

New

A special collection of official, beautifully detailed Harley-Davidson replicas from the Matchbox 1993 line. Each is specially decorated for this collector set. **Includes:** 1 Harley-Davidson Transporter, 2 Harley-Davidson Low Riders, 1 Harley-Davidson Hog, 1 Stunt Cycle, 1 Special Edition Patch, 1 Full Color Limited Edition Poster.

Standard Pack: 12
Carton Weight: 22 lbs.
Cube: 4.1
Package Size:
14" x 13" x 3"

Harley-Davidson® ELECTRA-GLIDE WITH SIDECAR

No. 76310

New

Collectors and Harley-Davidson® fans alike will be thrilled by this highly detailed, steerable diecast Electra-Glide model with sidecar and chromed features. Includes saddle bags, twin exhausts and engine detailing. Comes with rubber tires and real working suspension. Includes collector stand for display.

Standard Pack: 6
Carton Weight: 7.5 lbs.
Cube: 1.1
Package Size:
8" x 5⅝" x 7⁵⁄₃₂"

Tyco Toys, 1993, pg. 50

Harley-Davidson® ELECTRA-GLIDE

No. 76300

New

This classic, highly detailed 1/15 scale replica is a sure winner. With chromed features, saddle bags, and precision detailing. This cycle is steerable, comes with rubber tires, a working kickstand, and working suspension. Includes collector stand for display.

Standard Pack: 6
Carton Weight: 5.2 lbs.
Cube: .85
Package Size:
8" x 5⅝" x 5¹³⁄₃₂"

Harley-Davidson® SPORTSTER

No. 76330

New

The classic good looks of this 1/15 scale Sportster Bike are captured with this highly detailed bike. The Sportster Bike comes with rubber tires, real spring suspension, and a working kickstand. Includes collector stand for display.

Standard Pack: 6
Carton Weight: 5.5 lbs.
Cube: .85
Package Size:
8" x 5⅝" x 5¹³⁄₃₂"

Harley-Davidson® CAFE RACER

No. 76320

New

This authentic 1/15 scale diecast replica of a Harley Cafe Racer will be a sure favorite of all Harley fans. Authentic detailing, as well as steering, rubber tires, real spring suspension, and a working kickstand. Includes collector stand for display.

Standard Pack: 6
Carton Weight: 5.5 lbs.
Cube: .85
Package Size:
8" x 5⅝" x 5¹³⁄₃₂"

Tyco Toys, 1993, pg. 51

MATCHBOX MONSTER

MONSTER WARS

United States HOT ROD Association

Monster Wars is a one-hour, live-action syndicated TV show that is cleared in 65% of the U.S. Seen on weekends, Monster Wars combines live-action footage from Monster Truck racing events with story lines involving Super Hero Monster Wars characters. The "souls" of these trucks — represented by the Super Heroes — battle for the title of champion.

As Seen On Hit TV Show!

GRAVE DIGGER

PREDATOR

Tyco Toys, 1994, pg. 16

WARS BATTLE TRUCKS

As advertised on

TYCO® MATCHBOX

This is war! Monster Wars to be exact. Monster Wars combines the power and excitement of Monster Trucks with the personality and attitude of professional wrestling.

Monster Wars Battle Trucks   No. 35110   New

Monster Wars Battle Trucks are exact 1/43rd scale replicas of Grave Digger, Predator, Invader, and Equalizer — the same crushing bruisers you've seen battling each other on the USHRA circuit on TV. Each Monster Wars Battle Truck comes with a battle ram, articulated figure and battle accessories.

Standard Pack: 12 • **Carton Weight:** 6.3 lbs. • **Cube:** 1 • **Package Size:** 11" x 8⅛" blister card

Equalizer™

INVADER™

'MATCHBOX'
THUNDERBIRDS

Jeff

Hood

Scott

Virgil

Alan

Gordon

John

Brains

Parker

Lady Penelope

Thunderbirds Figures
41750

These highly detailed, 3 1/2" articulated figures include all the favorite Thunderbirds characters. Complete with individual accessories.

Standard Pack: 24 • **Carton Weight:** 6.6 lbs.
Cube: .4 • **Package Size:** 4⅞" x ¾ x 7⅞"

Thunderbird 1
41701

International Rescue's amazing scout ship, capable of traveling at 15,000 mph, is always the first Thunderbird on the scene.

Standard Pack: 24 • **Carton Weight:** 4.0 lbs.
Cube: 0.5 • **Package Size:** 5¹⁄₁₆" x 1¼" x 7⅞"

Thunderbird 3
41703

Thunderbird 3 is International Rescue's fully functional space shuttle, used to carry out daring rescues and communicate with satellites.

Standard Pack: 24 • **Carton Weight:** 4.0 lbs.
Cube: 0.5 • **Package Size:** 5¹⁄₁₆" x 1¼" x 7⅞"

Thunderbird 2 & 4
41702

Thunderbird 2 is the fantastic aircraft transporter capable of delivering an incredible variety of rescue vehicles right into the danger zone. Thunderbird 4 is a mini submarine, equipped with all the latest technology for underwater rescues.

Standard Pack: 12 • **Carton Weight:** 8.2 lbs.
Cube: 0.6 • **Package Size:** 10⅝" x 1⅝" x 7"

Tyco Toys, 1994, pg. 38

THUNDERBIRDS

Thunderbirds Rescue Gift Set
41700

Thunderbirds 1, 2, (and 4), 3 and FAB 1 — This complete gift set contains the entire diecast range, including the special edition of FAB 1, Lady Penelope's Rolls–Royce. The high-quality window box includes biographies on the Thunderbird team.

Standard Pack: 6 • **Carton Weight:** 8.8 lbs.
Cube: 8 • **Package Size:** 9⅜" x 1¾" x 12½"

Tracy Island Electronic Playset
41710

An exact replica of the Thunderbirds secret Tracy Island Headquarters. Open the hanger door and taxi out Thunderbird 2. Tilt the ramp (palm trees automatically fold down), lift the Blast Shield, and Thunderbird 2 is ready for launch. Slide back the swimming pool to reveal Thunderbird 1's secret launching silo. Thunderbird 3 launches through the Round House. This fully operational electronic playset comes with 4 pilot commands and realistic rocket sounds.

Standard Pack: 4
Carton Weight: 20.7 lbs.
Cube: 6.0
Package Size: 13½" x 8¼" x 20⅜"

Thunderbirds trademarks and copyrights used under license.

Tyco Toys, 1994, pg. 39

'MATCHBOX'®

GET IN THE FAST LANE!

SUPERFAST™

Assortment A No. 010774
Standard Pack: 144
Carton Weight: 22 lbs.
Cube: 1.5
Package Size: 4¼" x 6½"
blister card

New

Assortment B No. 019775
Standard Pack: 144
Carton Weight: 22 lbs.
Cube: 1.5
Package Size: 4¼" x 6½"
blister card

Win the Checkered Flag — Every Time! Hot New Look Keeps Blazing Through the Entire Line.

MORE COOL DESIGNS!

Look out for a wild fire of colorful racing action sweeping across the entire Matchbox® line.

With scorching speeds, the fastest - looking Matchbox® cars ever are pushing the entire "1-75" line to the extremes of motoring fun.

Racing for the pole position are 12 new models and 24 blazing new decos and more SuperFast™ cars than ever before!

The NEW MATCHBOX® LOOK sizzles in every segment!!!

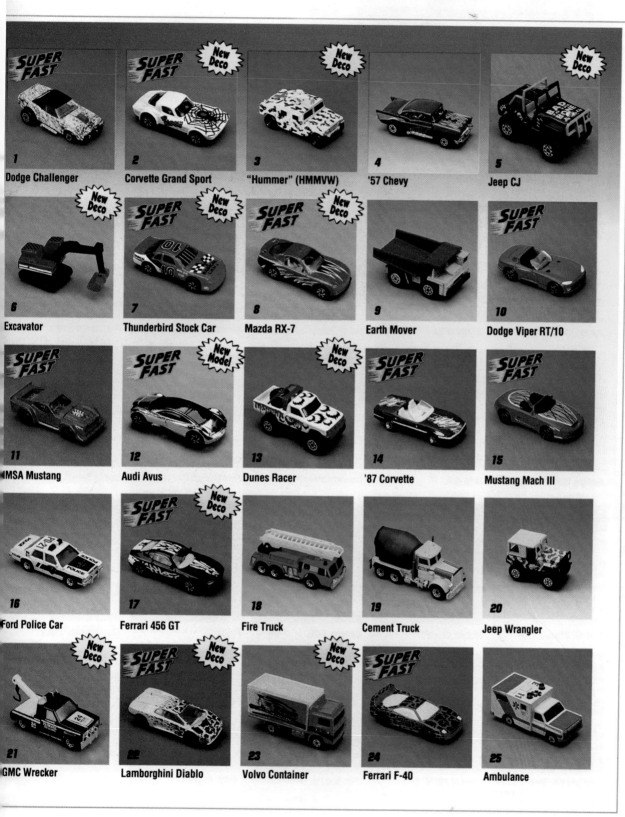

1 Dodge Challenger

2 Corvette Grand Sport

3 "Hummer" (HMMVW)

4 '57 Chevy

5 Jeep CJ

6 Excavator

7 Thunderbird Stock Car

8 Mazda RX-7

9 Earth Mover

10 Dodge Viper RT/10

11 IMSA Mustang

12 Audi Avus

13 Dunes Racer

14 '87 Corvette

15 Mustang Mach III

16 Ford Police Car

17 Ferrari 456 GT

18 Fire Truck

19 Cement Truck

20 Jeep Wrangler

21 GMC Wrecker

22 Lamborghini Diablo

23 Volvo Container

24 Ferrari F-40

25 Ambulance

Car Styling and Trademarks used under License or with Permission.

Tyco Toys, Spring 1995, pg. 21

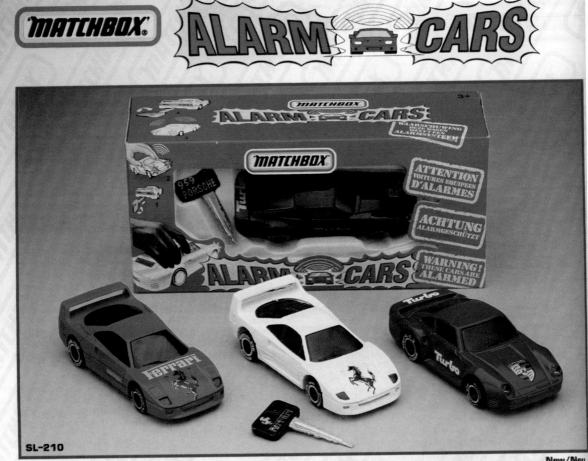

SL-210

Alarm Cars   **New/Neu**

Ferrari   **New/Neu**

Porsche 959   **New/Neu**

Alarm Cars

Warning These cars are alarmed. If you don't own the key, don't touch these cars–or else you'll get caught red handed.

Achtung: Diese Autos haben eine Alarmanlage. Wenn Du nicht den Schlüssel hast, versuche nicht sie zu stehlen, denn sonst wirst Du auf frischer Tat ertappt.

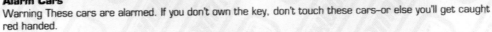

Matchbox, 1992

THUNDER MACHINES

LR-820

New/Neu

Thunder Machines

Thunder Machines

New key cars with a special electronic sound fob which "revs" the engine and listen to it peel out as it accelerates away!

Katapult–Autos mit Soundgenerator. Mit drei verschiedenen Geräuschen: Motor wird auf Touren gebracht, Startgeräusch, quietschende Reifen.

Matchbox, 1992

SUPERKINGS™

Matchbox 1988 Catalog, pg. 36

DAYS OF
Thunder ™

Capture the excitement and challenge of Days of Thunder™ racing with Matchbox racing cars and transports.

Experience the thrill of stock car competition at its best with collectible diecast race cars.

Race Car Asst.
(5 styles)
#32510 Pkd: 48

Race Car Challenge
(Twin Pk.)
#32520 Pkd: 24

Race Car Transporter
This car will not miss the race when transported by the authentically detailed transporter with matching race car! 2 styles.

#32630 Pkd: 24

Team Transporter
Exciting team racing transports are decorated with authentic detailing to move off your shelves! 5 styles.

#32560 Pkd: 24

Matchbox, Collector's Edition, 1991

DIECAST VEHICLES

16

MATCHBOX WORLD CLASS™

Lamborghini Countach

Ferrari 308 GTB

Porsche 928 S

Corvette Roadster

Series I

WORLD CLASS

Building on the 1989 success of the first World Class Series of vehicles, NEW for 1990, Matchbox introduces the World Class Series II Collection. World Class Series II will enhance the collection with the marks of Cadillac, Rolls Royce, BMW, Jaguar, Lincoln, and Thunderbird.

Our World Class vehicles are the ultimate in miniature diecast vehicles. Each highly detailed, high performance, diecast car features:

- Fully detailed tail lights and license plates
- Printed real rubber tires
- Metalized windows
- Authentic styling

Series I 1950
Series II 11700

Individual Package Size:
4¾" × 1½" × 8½"
Master Carton Size:
5" × 18¼" × 8¾"
Pack: 12
Weight: 3.5 lbs.
Cube: .46 cu. ft.

AM6 500 SEC Mercedes

Ferrari Testarossa

Porsche 944 Turbo

Porsche 959

Matchbox, 1990

DIECAST VEHICLES

17

MATCHBOX WORLD CLASS™

Jaguar XK120

Cadillac Allante

Lincoln Town Car

Series II

Rolls Royce Silver Cloud

Thunderbird Turbo Coupe

Ferrari F-40

Corvette Grand Sport

BMW/M1

Collector's Display Stand

COLLECTOR'S DISPLAY STAND

11750

This attractive display stand with a high gloss black finish is the perfect complement for 8 of our 16 World Class diecast vehicle collection. Our collector's stand is 11" high with eight removable clear platforms, each decorated with gold lettering and insignia recognizing each of the 16 World Class vehicles. The Matchbox World Class Collector's Display Stand will occupy pride of place on everyone's mantle.

Individual Package Size:
8¹⁵⁄₁₆" × 2¼" × 10⅞"

Master Carton Size:
13½" × 9¼" × 11¼"

Pack: 6

Weight: 4 lbs.

Cube: .83 cu. ft.

Matchbox, 1990

103

C O N N E C T A B L E S

NEW

THEMED CONNECTABLES

1902

New for 1990! Six new 5-section vehicles in popular recognizable themes that allow kids to create even more outrageous vehicles. Each themed vehicle includes a special section with moveable parts.

Individual Package Size:
7⅛″ × 10½″ × 1¼″

Master Carton Size:
7¼″ × 10¾″ × 21½″

Pack: 12

Weight: 5.75 lbs.

Cube: 1.17 cu. ft.

Themed Connectables interconnect to all existing and new Connectables products.

NEW

MICRO CONNECTABLES

71820

New for 1990! Now kids can create wacky Connectables vehicles in micro scale. The range consists of 18 new micro vehicles that are available in 8 packs of 6 sections.

Individual Package Size:
8½″ × 1½″ × 10½″

Master Carton Size:
18″ × 7½″ × 11″

Pack: 24

Weight: 8.65 lbs.

Cube: .23 cu. ft.

Micro Connectables interconnect to all existing and new Connectables products.

Matchbox, 1990

WORLD'S SMALLEST MATCHBOX

MAGNA-WHEEL
CARRY CASE

35370

All cities contain a variety of vehicles and the World's Smallest Matchbox city is no different from its real life counterparts.

The Magna-Wheel Carry Case and displays comes with and proudly displays 6 super detailed/super collectable World's Smallest Matchbox vehicles. Each vehicle sits in its own protective compartment. By rotating the clear display lid, a child can move the built in magnifying lens over the vehicle that he wants to get a closer look at. Only under magnification can one appreciate the extensive detailing of these highly miniaturized vehicles.

The Packs are:
- Exotics
- Sports
- Emergency
- Leisure

Individual Package Size:
8½" × 12½" × 1½"
Master Carton Size:
17" × 12½" × 12"
Pack: 24
Weight: 6.0 lbs.
Cube: 2.2 cu. ft.

Matchbox, 1990

MATCHBOX® Playsets

Matchbox Motors™

Car Wash™

Matchbox Collector's Edition, 1991

Matchbox Motors™

Just like a real car dealership! Elevator moves cars from the showroom to the rooftop service area. Drive down the ramp after repairs are done.

Item #550112 Pkd: 6

Car Wash™

Our Super Spin Car Wash actually washes and dries Matchbox vehicles. Manually operated conveyor moves vehicles through water jets, washing brushes and into the spin drier. Cars emerge sparkling clean!

Item #550117 Pkd: 6

Fold 'N Go™

Large self-contained fold up playsets in 2 very popular themes: 4-level parking and service garage. Each includes a variety of accessories and play features that fold up to go anywhere!

Asst. #50635 Pkd: 6

Main Street™

Large colorful playmat rolls up into case which forms a compact storage unit holding all accessories. Includes elevator, gates, lift, signs and lots more!

Item #1300 Pkd: 6

Matchbox Collector's Edition, 1991

NEW

LASER WHEELS™
ASST. 1000

Twelve high speed, hi-tech, high performance diecast vehicles. Each with low friction axles, the hot look of metal flake paint and laser image wheels.

Great design. Great look. These cars will get noticed!

Individual Pkg. Size: $8\frac{1}{2}$" x $4\frac{5}{8}$" x $2\frac{5}{16}$"

Master Carton Size: $10\frac{1}{4}$" x $9\frac{1}{2}$" x 28"

Pkd: 144

Wt. 21.75 lbs.

Cube: 1.56 cu. ft.

Matchbox 1988 Catalog, pg. 33

TYCO

6.0V JET TURBO® RADIO CONTROL TRUCK
with "Spitting" Dilophosaurus

SPITS WATER OVER 20 FEET BY RADIO CONTROL!

THE LOST WORLD
JURASSIC PARK

THE LOST WORLD: JURASSIC PARK™

Blaze the trails of The Lost World with 6.0V Jet Turbo® power!

Look Out! Cage breaks open on your command. . .

Dilophosaurus bursts out!

And spits water over 20 feet!

Standard Pack: 4
Weight: 13 lbs.
Cube: 2.1
Package Size: 8½" x 12¼" x 7¾"

6.0V Jet Turbo® The Lost World: Jurassic Park Radio Control Truck
With Radio Control "Spitting" Dilophosaurus!

No. 2866

New!

Tackle the darkest corners of The Lost World: Jurassic Park! Tyco's new 6.0V Jet Turbo R/C Truck goes anywhere and carries a lurking surprise in back! Look Out! Push the special transmitter button and Dilophosaurus "breaks" open his cage, springs up, and spits a stream of water 20 feet. . . all by your radio control command! Vehicle features 6.0 V Jet Turbo speed and power, with full-function steering, forward, and reverse controls. Rechargeable 6.0 V Jet Turbo NiCd Battery Pack and 9 volt alkaline required. Not included.

Tyco Toys, 1997, pg. 53

Resources

The private collection of Mr. Dana Johnson, Bend, Oregon.

The private collection of Mr. Dan Rickards, Bend, Oregon.

American Wheels, A Reference, by Jerry Rettig, published by ELC, copyright 2000.

Diecast Cars of the 1960s, Mac Ragan, MBI Publishing Company (Motor Books International), ISBN 0760307199, copyright 2000.

Die Cast Price Guide, Post-War: 1946 – Present, Douglas R. Kelly, Antique Trader Books, ISBN 0930625277, copyright 1997.

The Encyclopedia of Matchbox Toys, Revised & Expanded 3rd Edition, Charlie Mack, Schiffer Publishing, ISBN 0764315714, copyright 2002.

Matchbox and Lledo Toys, Dr. Edward Force, Schiffer Publishing, ISBN 0887401279, copyright 1988.

Matchbox Cars, Mac Ragan, MBI Publishing Company (Motor Books International), ISBN 0760309647, copyright 2002.

Matchbox Toys, Revised 5th Edition, Nancy Schiffer, Schiffer Publishing, ISBN 0764309919, copyright 2000.

Miniature Emergency Vehicles, Dr. Edward Force, Schiffer Publishing, ISBN 0887400310, copyright 1985.

O'Brien's Collecting Toy Cars & Trucks, Identification & Value Guide, 3rd Edition, edited by Elizabeth Stephan, Krause Publications, copyright 2000.

Standard Encyclopedia of Die-Cast Vehicles, Identification and Values, edited by Dan Stearns, Krause Publications, ISBN 0873494199, copyright 2002.

Today's Hottest Die-Cast Vehicles, edited by Elizabeth A. Stephan, Krause Publications, ISBN 0873419189, copyright 2000.

Other Books by Dana Johnson

Also available from Collector Books

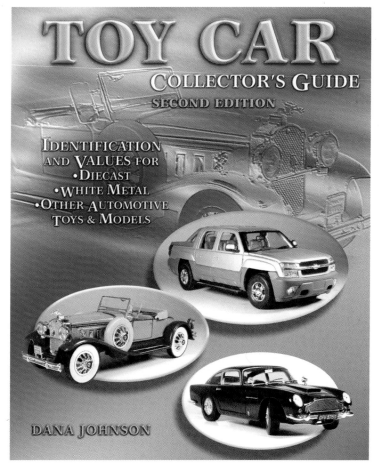

8½" x 11", PB, $24.95, 416 pgs.

Toy Car Collector's Guide, Second Edition

Dana Johnson, author of *Matchbox Toys, 1947 to 2003, Fourth Edition, The Other Matchbox Toys,* and *Diecast Toys & Scale Models*, has produced a revised edition of his popular *Toy Car Collector's Guide.* Newly updated and expanded, this second edition provides an alphabetical listing by brand of nearly 1,000 brands of cast iron, tinplate, diecast, slush mold, plastic, white metal, and other toy cars from around the world and through automotive history. An estimated 50,000 models are represented, including brief company profiles of every brand. Over 1,300 color photographs serve to greatly enhance the exhaustive text of this all-inclusive book, undoubtedly the most comprehensive on the market.

Matchbox Toys, 1947 to 2003, Fourth Edition

Our fourth edition of *Matchbox Toys* is the most user-friendly Matchbox collector's guide ever produced. While most publications on this subject are organized by model number or year of introduction, Dana Johnson's book is arranged alphabetically by model name and description. No more will you have to flip page after page hunting for the car you're looking for — this book makes location a snap! Well over 1,000 photographs are included in this latest edition, with multiple variations pictured of selected models, all incorporated into a cohesive guide to early Lesney models, the Matchbox basic (1-75) series, Matchbox Collectibles, and more.

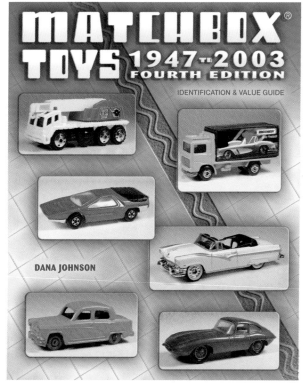

COLLECTOR BOOKS
P.O. Box 3009, Paducah, KY 42002–3009
1-800-626-5420
www.collectorbooks.com

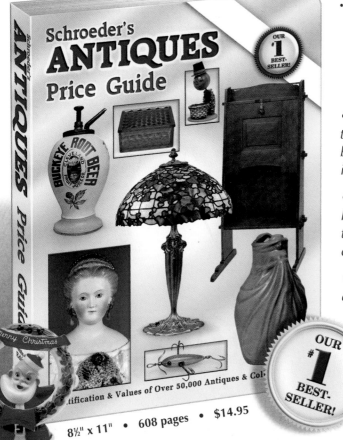